MEMOIRS FROM THE VEIL

TRANS-DIMENSIONAL EXPERIENCES
IN EVERYDAY LIFE

Ronald W. Lawrence

BALBOA.
PRESS
A DIVISION OF HAY HOUSE

Copyright © 2018 Ronald W. Lawrence.

All rights reserved. No part of this book may be used or reproduced by any means, graphic, electronic, or mechanical, including photocopying, recording, taping or by any information storage retrieval system without the written permission of the author except in the case of brief quotations embodied in critical articles and reviews.

Balboa Press books may be ordered through booksellers or by contacting:

Balboa Press
A Division of Hay House
1663 Liberty Drive
Bloomington, IN 47403
www.balboapress.com
1 (877) 407-4847

Because of the dynamic nature of the Internet, any web addresses or links contained in this book may have changed since publication and may no longer be valid. The views expressed in this work are solely those of the author and do not necessarily reflect the views of the publisher, and the publisher hereby disclaims any responsibility for them.

The author of this book does not dispense medical advice or prescribe the use of any technique as a form of treatment for physical, emotional, or medical problems without the advice of a physician, either directly or indirectly. The intent of the author is only to offer information of a general nature to help you in your quest for emotional and spiritual well-being. In the event you use any of the information in this book for yourself, which is your constitutional right, the author and the publisher assume no responsibility for your actions.

Any people depicted in stock imagery provided by Getty Images are models, and such images are being used for illustrative purposes only.
Certain stock imagery © Getty Images.

Editors
Dennis Mc Bride, Daniel C. Hinkley

Illustrations
Aaronell Matta

Cover Design
Daniel C. Hinkley
Nathan Uhlir

Cover Graphic
Nathan Uhlir

Print information available on the last page.

ISBN: 978-1-9822-1391-6 (sc)
ISBN: 978-1-9822-1392-3 (hc)
ISBN: 978-1-9822-1393-0 (e)

Library of Congress Control Number: 2018912009

Balboa Press rev. date: 10/09/2018

This book is dedicated to all who have had the courage to share their trans-dimensional experiences and know beyond doubt that they are real.

CONTENTS

NOTE

In order to protect the confidentiality of the individuals who have unique experiences, identities and experiences have been fictionalized. Only the universal trans-dimensional experiences that exist as core truths have been mentioned as they universally occur worldwide. From time to time those universal core experiences have appeared in my life.

INTRODUCTION

When I was a small child, my mother was conscientious about putting me down for a nap in the afternoon. What happened to me during one of those afternoon nap times when I was about four years old is an experience I have remembered all my life.

My favorite store in our small town of Turtle Creek, Pennsylvania was the G.C. Murphy Five and Dime Store. After my mother went grocery shopping at the A & P market across the street, she would take me over to G.C. Murphy's. There was always a bag of candy and a comic book to take home. One afternoon my mother put me down for my nap and I had what I thought then was a dream. In my "dream" I found myself heading for the Five and Dime. As I traveled along the street my way was blocked by a passing bus. Suddenly I was on the bus hovering in the center aisle. It was late afternoon rush hour when the local factory had dismissed the afternoon shift of office workers, so the bus was crowded and buzzing with conversation. At that time, people smoked more than they do today and the bus was filled with a white haze of cigarette smoke. I remember how fashionably the bus passengers were dressed.

I observed in particular a small, attractive woman and hovered above her left shoulder. She wore a grey business suit with a thin white stripe and shoulder pads, which was common in 1940s women's fashion. Her hat was black velvet and she was having a casual conversation with the person sitting next to her.

And that was it. I found myself back in my body in my bed at home. It was not till many years later when I was an adult and had studied trans-dimensional phenomena that I realized the dream that I had experienced when I was a child was actually an out-of-body experience, and that I was "remote viewing" on that bus.

The career I chose when I grew up (in my forties) was in the field of psychotherapy: marital and family therapy, and clinical psychology. In 1990 I co-founded the Community Counseling Center in Las Vegas. During the ensuing decades I counseled hundreds of patients, many of whom admitted, often reluctantly, various paranormal and trans-dimensional experiences similar to what I had experienced as a four-year-old. I learned how widespread such experiences are. And in continuing and upgrading my formal education, I also learned that the education system can be somewhat hostile to these experiences and toward those who share them.

One of my favorite professors was "Dr. John." We agreed about society's need for healing and our personal and professional connection was powerful. John was an engaging teacher who inspired me to understand what it means to be alive and interacting on this earth. In 1996 I published privately a small memoir in honor of my dear friend, Jerry Chestnut, who died of HIV-related illness in 1994. *Sharing the Light* detailed my metaphysical experiences surrounding Jerry's death. I sent a copy of the book to John who appreciated and praised my experience, and told me, "In so many ways we're on the same page and understand that there's more to life than what we can see, feel, and touch." Visiting him at home one afternoon he took me to his library, and pointed to a shelf of neatly arranged books on spirituality, metaphysics, and extra-sensory phenomena, including Shirley MacLaine's famous memoir, *Out on a Limb*. "These are some of the books I would love to have in the classroom," John said. "But I can't. It would never be accepted." I found it sad that a teacher as fine as John possessed a world of knowledge and wisdom that he could not share to benefit his students for fear of being shamed and ridiculed. Nevertheless, John's reticence validated my own search for truth and understanding.

Some years later I invited an individual to conduct training at Community Counseling Center. This teacher was prominent and respected in her field. When one of the psychotherapists in class questioned her regarding an odd and obviously trans-dimensional experience of one of her patients, she cut her off. "We don't talk about those things," she said. "They can't be placed in a test tube or measured in a laboratory, so what's the point?"

That denial is still the basic position of the mental health teaching and treatment field. In refusing to validate the fact there are trans-dimensional experiences in human life, something significant is missing from treatment and connection with the populations that we serve. Talking about, studying, and teaching such phenomena as the empathic near-death experience that I shared with my friend Jerry, discussed later in this book, add legitimacy and meaning to our human journey. As I near total retirement and consider all the trans-dimensional experiences my clients and friends have shared with me—and which I have experienced myself–I'm determined to bring this knowledge out of the closet. John was correct in noting that "there's more to life than what we can see, feel, and touch."

* * *

ONE

"Not everything we experience can be explained by logic or science." Linda Westphal

Dissociative Experiences: Opening Windows into Other Dimensions

On April 1, 1990, together with three colleagues, I founded Community Counseling Center of Southern Nevada. Community Counseling is an addiction and mental health recovery service whose main outreach, initially, was to people living with HIV disease who were having difficulty receiving services from an uninformed and fearful community. Because of the discrimination I had seen and experienced in my own life as a gay man, I worked hard to assure that our agency was open to all. As agency director I had to manage such daunting tasks as dealing with bureaucracies and searching out funding sources. As a psychotherapist I had a full caseload of vulnerable patients in physical, emotional, and spiritual need. After years of academic training I was able to assist with meeting my patients' physical and emotional needs through treatment and referral. Their spiritual need was another matter.

I'm not a scientist, nor am I a religious person. I was not aware of other dimensions or that there are windows between this dimension and what I now believe to be a "next" one. Despite my own experiences, I could not wrap my mind around metaphysical concepts. I had no spiritual vocabulary. But as years passed and I worked to help and heal my patients, my friends and myself, our mutual experiences became my teachers and opened doors for me into a world that is both spiritual and trans-dimensional. Over time my consciousness transformed and the

1

conventional dogmas that I believed in turned to dust and blew away. I think of myself today as a spiritual person. I've learned a great deal from the wonderful souls I've counseled and others that I've experienced in life, and have much to share about their experiences and mine.

One of my first teachers was a patient I'll call John. He was a bright thirty-five-year-old who reminded me of a young Kirk Douglass. John was stymied by this "relationship thing" and sought my assistance. His intent was to cultivate skills that would lead the way to a meaningful and healthy partnership with someone. After several weeks in therapy, he suddenly asked me, "Did I ever tell you about my out-of-body experience?"

"No," I said. "But I'm listening." Our time together in therapy led John to trust that I would take his story seriously.

"My leg was a mess," he told me. "It had been broken. And I finally needed surgery. I was on the operating table and under anesthesia. All of a sudden, I was somehow floating above the scene and looking down at myself. The experience seemed to happen in a split second. I was watching the surgeon work. I noticed that the first thing he did was make an incision right below my knee. One of the assistants wiped some blood as it ran over to my right. Then the doctor seemed to do some scraping on the bone in the open area. The assistant cleaned the area as the surgery proceeded. Then the surgeon seemed to take some kind of a reading. I went back into my body. The assistant came in to check on me when I was in recovery," John continued. "I explained to him that I was seeing their handiwork from above and looking down at the procedure. I asked about the instrument they were using to take some kind of reading. He looked at me with disbelieving eyes, almost telling me that he didn't want to hear it. But I explained what I witnessed at the beginning of the procedure. He nodded and with raised eyebrows told me my account was accurate."

John wanted to understand his experience and sought explanation. My only tool then was to tell him that he was not alone, that while I didn't have an explanation for what happened, many people claim similar experiences.

"If you could assign an explanation," I asked, "what is it that you would say happened?"

"I think my spirit left my body and that I was somehow seeing myself from the outside. And I think that if anyone doubts that we have a spirit, they're just wrong!"

"That's probably as good an explanation as any," I added. At that time, I had no way of offering anything deeper or more precise.

John definitely had an out-of-body experience—but science mostly dismisses experiences it can't explain or tries to place it in a test tube of some sort. But I believe that such experiences have a wide latitude. Some of them break the paradigm of science-based logic and are labeled as hallucinations. In this case, it would be called an autoscopic hallucination. But I firmly disagree with that label, especially in cases where the patient brings back factual observations that are gleaned when out-of-body, as John had. I intend to share my own theories and ideas about these experiences and what they mean.

The most important concept to consider is "dissociation." *The Encyclopedia of Mental Disorders*[1] defines dissociation as "a mechanism that allows the mind to separate or compartmentalize certain memories or thoughts from normal consciousness." Since the word "mind" appears in this definition, I turn to Dr. Daniel Siegel and his article entitled, "Mindsight: The New Science of Personal Transformation."[2]

In his article, Siegel defines mind as "a regulatory process that can be monitored, measured, observed and modified." The brain is an organ very much like a computer with storage capacity. Mind is the organizing principle –the "program"–that calls up memories that are stored in the brain, as well as other information and associations. As the organizer, the mind places information into concepts and categories. I attended a speech at a training event in December 2013. [3] After discussing the concept of mind, in an eloquent way, a trainer held his finger to his forehead and reminded the audience that mind does not end there. The psychotherapists from eighteen countries burst into applause. "We all know it," I thought. "And thanks for the validation!" We may, however, lack the vocabulary to fully explain why mind doesn't end at the forehead.

I believe dissociation is the partial separation of mind from the physical body that produces an alternate state of consciousness, and it involves all the physical and spiritual constructs that we possess: Body; Brain; Mind; Consciousness; and what is known as the Torsion Field; Energy Body; Soul. A person experiencing dissociation feels the separation from their body to varying degrees, and is aware of information they may not know when they are in normal, waking consciousness. I call attention to this concept and experience because it provides a view through the veil that separates our physical plane of existence from the next dimension.

Lately, however, I've learned there's more to dissociation than simple separation of mind/consciousness from the body. Although they are controversial, I support theories brought forward by Russian scientist A. Akimov[4] and American physicist Claude Swanson[5]. Their research describes what they call torsion fields, which are subtle energy fields. The concept of this phenomenon has been known for a long time. Western science has taken delight, however, in mostly debunking the concept and even labeling its theorists as detached from reality. Notable individuals such as Wilhelm Reich[6] discussed the possibility of a subtle energy field and were ridiculed by mainstream science. Biologist Rupert Sheldrake refers to these subtle energy fields as morphic fields. In his article, "Morphic Fields – An Introduction," [7] Sheldrake writes, "Morphic fields underlie our mental activity and our perceptions. The morphic fields of social groups connect members of the group even when they are many miles apart. They help provide an explanation for telepathy."

Akimov describes our brain as "a vacuum-based torsion field transceiver." Torsion fields are waves of energy that also carry information. This means that when the field is activated we can both send and receive information. In addition, I believe that the torsion field has trans-dimensional qualities. Akimov believes that torsion field energy travels much faster than the speed of light, and that it can also have a physical influence over something in an environment, even in remote locations. This is the concept behind remote viewing—"seeing" something that's far away from one's physical location–and remote influence–physically influencing an object from a distance.

I was mowing my lawn one evening when an image of my patient, Frank, flashed into my consciousness. I thought to myself, "I wonder how he's doing?" Not two seconds later I ran inside the house to answer the phone. It was my answering service with Frank holding on the line. He was experiencing a crisis and his torsion field, activated by his heightened emotions, had reached me before his telephone call.

Heightened states of consciousness prompt super-charging of torsion field energy. The propensity for activation varies from one person to another. While Native Americans may not have known what to call it, they knew it existed. During World War II our military recognized the prowess of Native American scouts and invited them to participate in various strategic activities. Their ability to "see ahead," report information, and sense danger or safety was amazing. In more primitive times, activation of the torsion field provided information that related to the survival of the tribe. As humanity moved into more mechanized and highly technological societies, this indigenous wisdom was discarded as being similar to superstition.

Before I describe more experiences that cause us to dissociate, I want to discuss consciousness. Dean Radin, in his book, *The Conscious Universe*, discusses the properties of consciousness :[8]

1. Consciousness extends beyond the individual and has quantum field-like properties in that it affects the probabilities of events.

2. Consciousness injects order into systems in proportion to the "strength" of consciousness present.

3. The strength of consciousness in an individual fluctuates from moment to moment and is regulated by focus of attention.

4. A group of individuals can be said to have "group consciousness." Group consciousness strengthens when the group's attention is focused on an object or an event and this creates coherence among the group.

5. When individuals in a group are all attending different things, then the group consciousness and group mental coherence is effectively zero producing what amounts to background noise.

6. Physical systems of all kinds respond to a consciousness field by becoming more ordered. The stronger or more coherent a consciousness field, the more order will be evident.

Radin's description of consciousness suggests the question; is consciousness what has long been referred to as soul? We have an energy body that is quite visible with Kirlian photography. I believe this may reflect the spirit part of us, the "soul" that moves on when we die, and it may well be the torsion field that serves as the vehicle for soul travel.

Kendra Cherry, in her article "Consciousness: The Psychology of Awareness," gives a more prosaic definition.[9] "Consciousness," she writes, "refers to your individual awareness of your unique thoughts, memories, feelings, sensations, and environment. Your conscious experiences are constantly shifting and changing." I will add that there are *states* of consciousness. There's a certain state when we're sad and another when we're running a marathon. Each state has an impact on what and how we perceive. When we're depressed such a state can color all of our perceptions. As we experience awareness, perceptions are organized by our mind and stored in the brain. Human consciousness and the subtle energy of the torsion field are intimately connected. The information-carrying torsion field feeds data through our consciousness which then gets organized by our mind and recorded in the brain.

I believe that most dissociative experiences involve body, mind, and spirit. Part of us separates from the body to some degree. The mind, or part of it, travels with our consciousness, organizes the experience and sends information back to the brain to store as memories. And if we dissociate deeply, we can cross the boundary that takes us to the next dimension of existence. We look through or pass through a window that separates this dimension from the next.

Dissociation is often caused by a profoundly disturbing or dangerous event such as a near-death experience where a person sees loved ones who have died and/or angelic beings who urge the individual to return to this dimension. These beings occasionally state reasons why the person should return, reasons that often come to fruition after returning.

When my friend, Andrea, was giving birth, her natural birth process was long, difficult and exhausting. In spite of her youth and strength, she experienced cardiac arrest at the very end of the delivery. She— her spirit–floated up near the ceiling of the delivery room. The scene below was clearly visible to her. She could see her husband standing outside the circle of medical personnel in tears, trembling and pacing as staff members worked frantically to revive her. And then, her spirit traveled a bit farther from the scene. According to her report, the scene below seemed to shrink away as though being viewed from far away. In the flash of a second, an image of her mother, who had died unexpectedly a year before–appeared directly in front of her. Her expression reflected unconditional love. While she didn't actually speak, her message was clear: "You must go back. The child will need you!" The next thing Andrea remembered was being back in her body, gasping for breath.

When Andrea went into cardiac arrest in the delivery room, trauma supercharged her torsion field. Even though part of her was separated from her body, the experience of being "out" was relayed back to her brain including the trans-dimensional experience of seeing her mother and receiving her message. In addition to her new-born child, Andrea's journey into motherhood contained an unexpected spiritual experience.

She attests that it changed her life and has been the source of her spiritual awakening.

Dr. Sam Parnia of the University of Southampton conducted one of the largest studies of near-death experiences to date.[10] The study, involving over two thousand participants, indicates that in the first few moments after death, consciousness is not annihilated. Some individuals have returned to the living with accurate descriptions of events around them when they were in the out-of-body state. Andrea's descriptions of the delivery room scene were accurate.

This sense of separation caused by dissociation is protective when we experience trauma. Our consciousness and mental processes shift to the task of physical survival and the processing of emotions is postponed until we feel safe. As we experience the emotional intensity of trauma the torsion field may activate more powerfully and provide us with an out-of-body view of what's happening, or of ourselves in the event. And many times, when a trigger event or reminder occurs in front of a post-traumatic individual, the possibility of dissociating is strong. We are physically anchored to this reality while reliving a past experience— we are in two places at once. Processing with a trained professional in psychotherapy can reduce symptoms and disempower the trigger's influence. Once the mind/body has the experience of dissociation, however, the process may happen more easily with new traumatic experiences or, as some patients have reported to me, they can dissociate and have experiences, such as out-of-body, at will.

Tommy, was viciously abused to the point of dissociation in a manufacturing setting when he was a child. Just the smell of glue was the trigger that caused him to dissociate as an adult, thus activating his torsion field. As he described, "I may be sitting someplace where the smell of glue, all of a sudden, permeates the air, but once the smell comes, my spirit self is outside in the parking lot. I feel safer there." But Tommy's brain remembers the parking lot experience and he can relate to what happened there while his physical self was inside.

Regarding traumatic memories themselves, which can prompt dissociation, my patients have been mystified by the fact that when they have a new trauma they re-experience many of the traumatic memories that they experienced in the past. The great psychiatrist, Milton Erickson, explained this phenomenon concisely when he said, referring to emotional states, "Memories are state dependent."[11] When we arrive at a certain emotional state, everything that's stored in memory that's similar in feeling can resurface at the conscious level. We re-experience feelings and images.

Years ago I experienced the sudden death of a team member at my place of employment. Living with the shock of that experience, it's as though I was encountering emotions and memories of every death that I ever experienced that occurred close to me. All of a sudden, I re-experienced my grandma's funeral, both waking and in dreams. When I went into the emotional state of loss, perhaps even shock, I became flooded with memories of the past that bore the same reflection.

My good friend, Sally, was driving on icy roads one cold morning. She always exercised caution in her small compact car because there wasn't much metal around her for protection. Another auto appeared in front of her and she spontaneously hit the brakes. She knew that regardless of any action taken, she was going to hit the car in front of her. It was inevitable and unstoppable. For a split second, flooded with fear, Sally was outside of her body viewing herself from above. Her spirit self was out in the torsion field, which she remembered later. Once the collision was over, Sally was back into her physical body feeling a rush of emotion. Seeing herself from above was a mysterious and frightening experience. "Was I preparing to die?" she asked me. "No," I explained. "It was your mind/body's way of providing a moment of protection. You saw what was happening but didn't feel anything until you were back in your body." *ME*

Nightmares are their own special category of trauma. Dreams have been studied ever since human beings have experienced consciousness. Nightmares can be the reliving of an unresolved trauma complete with accurate images. They can also be simply the feelings from the trauma with non-matching images. Or perhaps they're a seed that's been planted in the unconscious that was inspired by a story, a movie, or an image that crossed our perceptions. Regardless of their origin, nightmares can cause dissociation and result in out-of-body experiences. Individuals can leave their bodies during sleep due to sheer fright and have recollections of floating above. They may also awaken once they re-enter their body with complete recollection including their feelings of fright.

My own dissociation due to nightmares occurred as a child. When I was in first grade my grandfather treated me to Tarzan movies on Saturday afternoons. Johnny Weissmuller was quite the hero, but the lions and tigers were scary. One night I had a dream that some beast was in pursuit and I was running away from it. I was petrified with fear, and in the dream I opened my mouth to scream, but I couldn't. It was that feeling that took me out of my body. I remember floating out of my room and hovering in the hallway of our house. At the other end of the hall I saw a white, shapeless entity. There was enough shape that I could clearly see a head. My feeling now is that whoever or whatever it was, they were there to help and comfort. Not understanding what was happening to me, I felt a second flood of terror. Suddenly, I was back in my body and awoke. Then, I could scream! My father came running. Through my hyperventilation and tears, I told him I'd seen Casper, the ghost. I had no way of explaining an out-of-body experience. Nor did I understand that my torsion field could relay information about the trans-dimensional experience of seeing an entity while out-of-body.

Shock is an emotional sub-category that is part of trauma. It's often the first part of working through a traumatic experience. Something happens that drastically changes the nature of our reality. Some symptoms of shock are denial, disbelief, confusion, and numbness. Brain chemistry and functions will change.

A person who once worked closely with me was out jogging. He had a massive heart attack and died on the road where he was running. Just the day before, we had planned a hiking trip on the upcoming weekend. For several days I had a sense of unreality. My perceptions changed and I had a heightened sense of acuity. The whole issue of mortality was constantly on my mind. I wondered, "Could this happen to me?" As I tried processing this experience, my personal priorities changed. Things that once seemed important lost their place on my internal lists. I certainly dissociated but didn't exactly have a word for it. People in shock will say, "I don't feel like myself," because their state of being is so surreal. The shock eventually breaks. Feelings and expressions can flow again. The memories of being in that place are always there and a little piece of our existence may be changed forever in some way.

Another experience that can lead to dissociation is heavy drug or alcohol abuse. There are times when individuals partake so deeply that they experience a degree of separation. A patient whom I will call Alex was a former heroin addict. During his days as a heavy user, he had out-of-body experiences. He remembered administering the drug one day and becoming semi-conscious. At one point, he found himself looking down at his anesthetized body. He remembered seeing himself limp and lifeless. His sense of knowing told him that he was in an alternate state, which he didn't understand. His spiritual self floated out of his bedroom and down the hallway in his home until he reached the door that led outside. Suddenly, he had an overwhelming sense of fright. He remembered the exact thought that he had in that moment: "I'm dying!" In a split second, he was back in his body struggling to open his eyes and move. It was the fear of having taken himself to the edge that inspired Alex to initiate an addiction recovery process. His experience was living proof that journeys of consciousness can lead us to healing and insight.

Some of us, like patient Alex, have immediate recall of a dissociative experience. In cases of deep trauma, however, accompanied by amnesia, memories of dissociation don't resurface until recall of the event appears. Sometimes recall happens in a split second due to a trigger in the environment. Sometimes recall happens in animated, sometimes frightening, flashbacks. Recall can also surface during hypnosis or meditation. When the torsion field is more activated, memory of the experience is sent to the brain. If a person fails to understand the experience because they have no frame of reference for it, the mystery is often solved in psychotherapy. Patients will ask me, "Why was I seeing myself from above?"

I believe that part of the energy of consciousness lives outside the body. We can see this energy body in the shape of an aura in Kirlian photography. I feel that when someone dissociates, the torsion field activates, generated by the neurons in our brain. Consciousness relays information from the more mobile torsion field to the mind to be recorded in the brain as memories. My patients often have mentioned the existence of a cord, rope, or string that keeps them connected to their body. The ultimate dissociative experience is death. When we die, I believe that the consciousness and spiritual essence—the connecting cord–are completely severed from the physical self and we (the soul) move into the "next" dimension.

Dissociation is not always a result of trauma, however. These experiences can be positive and soothing. This is "positive dissociation." Deep meditation is a perfect example. During my meditation training, my awareness changed dramatically. While focused on thinking and breathing and repeating my mantra over and over, I was barely aware that I had a body. My chattering and ruminative mind quieted, my body secreted endorphins, I relaxed mentally, and a change in my consciousness occurred. My torsion field activated and "hunches" about things outside myself clarified. I also noticed perceptual and cognitive changes as I moved more deeply into the meditative process. I seemed to move out of the reality that I had lived in all my life, and suddenly had a "wider" view of humanity and the world, a more expansive perspective. I felt that my compassion had increased and my intuition became fine-tuned. I could engage with the essence of my practice of psychotherapy much more deeply. As a therapist, part of my job is to reflect the life process back to my patients. More than once, after I had offered a succinct theory to a patient regarding their personal process, I was asked, "Are you psychic?" My answer would be, "No, just fine-tuned."

As we move in and out of meditative states—and sleep, for that matter—our brain waves and brain activity change. This is a primary factor in psychic experiences as well as experiences related to what we call spirit or soul. This understanding is important in exploring all the variables that occur around and within dissociative experiences.

* * *

TWO

"Our eternal spiritual self is more real than anything we perceive in this physical realm, and has a divine connection to the infinite love of the Creator."
Eben Alexander MD

Variables

My internship in graduate school taught me many things. As I noted earlier, traumatic events often lead to post-traumatic stress–stress after the event. Acute stress is more about what happens in the immediacy. Many of these experiences are accompanied by dissociation.

When I began my psychotherapy practice in Las Vegas, one of my first patients was Walter, a military veteran. As he described his symptoms and problems, it was obvious Walt had full-blown post-traumatic stress disorder due to heavy combat situations. He had nightmares and flashbacks that destabilized his life as a husband, father, and employee. Depression was part of his everyday life. He would leave his family and sleep up in the mountains for days. "What's wrong with me?" he asked.

"You're experiencing classic post-traumatic stress disorder," I explained.

He pondered. "So, the word *disorder* means I'm crazy?"

"Let's rephrase that," I suggested. "You're having a post-traumatic experience."

"Then, I'm not crazy?"

"No," I said. "These are normal experiences that many people have when exposed to frightening and traumatic events." Walt's treatment proceeded productively after that conversation. It taught me, however, to be very cautious about using the word "disorder." Should we call them disorders when they are protective experiences which offer a way to cope with difficult situations? I believe these are normal experiences for people who have walked through terror.

The American Psychiatric Association [APA], in the fifth publication of the *Diagnostic and Statistical Manual*, lists several dissociative "disorders."[12] These phenomena reflect the separation-from-self symptoms that occur when we're under severe stress or experiencing trauma. When they occur they are often accompanied by some kind of trans-dimensional experience. This means that our consciousness travels to a different dimension other than the one in which we live which contains length, breadth, and depth. Individuals who have had a dissociative experience will often claim they have a more powerful intuition and sharper perceptions that are more fine-tuned than before the event that caused them to dissociate.

Significantly, part of the list of dissociative "disorders" defined by the APA is Dissociative Identity Disorder [DID], a new name for Multiple Personality. One of my teachers classified it as a "psycho-spiritual disorder." Dropping the word "disorder," we can say it's a "psycho-spiritual experience." Briefly, when a person experiences intensifying levels of trauma, certain breaking points appear when the experiencer may feel that death is imminent. Or, it may be that the mind/body has reached some internal experiential limit. At these points, a new identity will develop in order to endure each escalation point in the trauma. Barriers of amnesia are formed between the various identities. A pre-treatment dissociative identity person will often have separate identities that have no idea the others are even there. I often refer to that cluster of phenomena as "dissociative identity in the raw." Symptoms will include lost time. What happened between 2:00 PM and 6:00 PM? Who was in charge of the body at that time? Or, one might "wake up" in the middle of some experience or conversation and have to adlib one's way through it. Identities will reappear with the introduction of certain cues and triggers in the environment, especially if those cues serve as a reminder of a specific past trauma. These dissociative individuals are usually endowed with magnificent survival skills. They can also be extremely psychic and even exhibit psycho-kinetic abilities—able to move objects with their mind because their torsion fields are extremely active.

The next APA diagnosis is Dissociative Amnesia.[12] Persons having this experience fail to remember all or part of their own identity and life experience. Some extremely traumatic memory is usually seething under the surface. In these moments, known as dissociative fugues, a person cannot remember who they are and where they belong, and they will often wander to distant destinations. The dissociated person who is separated from self is often the one who peers through the window in the veil between dimensions and gleans pertinent information relevant to past, present, or future. Their subtle energy torsion field is "lit up." As with DID, their disclosures are often labeled as delusion, confusion, or sometimes invalidated in treatment.

Depersonalization/De-realization Disorder is next in the APA dissociative diagnoses.[12] Depersonalization is described as a sense of unreality, detachment, or being an outside observer to one's own thoughts, feelings, sensations, body, and actions. My friend, Arnie, as a teenager, confessed he had gay feelings, so his fundamentalist Christian church went to work on him. They scared the living daylights out of him with threats of God's wrath and going to hell. He was having terrifying nightmares of being in hell and having fire all around him. Arnie had been living with terrible dissonance. Part of him loved his male partner and another part of him felt that he was damned for his relationship.

Bringing such years-long trauma to the surface can serve as a path to healing–but recalling the trauma often will ignite a dissociative experience. Arnie and his spouse had been vacationing in California. On their way home, they had driven past an area that had a raging forest fire in the distance. The image served as a cue for what Arnie's dreams reflected in regard to burning in hell. During the remainder of the drive home, Arnie found himself depersonalizing. "I was driving my car," he recalled. "But I felt like there was someone else doing it! It's as though I wasn't there." Spending time with one of my peers in a therapeutic intervention brought Arnie back to himself.

De-realization can feel bizarre. This is a sense of unreality or detachment with respect to one's surroundings. A patient told me, "I'm here. I know I'm here. Yet I feel like I'm somewhere else." When my friend, Jerry, died after his long battle with illness, I was bedside at his final moments. I knew Jerry was going to die but finally experiencing his loss drove me to dissociate. I sat with his body quietly after he passed while waiting for the mortuary. The hospital room became "thick." When I moved, I felt like the atmosphere was heavy. It was as though life had become a slow-motion movie. When I looked at Jerry's face, he seemed to be smiling. Did my dissociation contain an element of delusion? Was I seeing only what I wanted to see? I looked again. There was no smile, just peace.

My sense of de-realization continued for hours. When I arrived at home, my spouse, Daniel, did his best to comfort me. He pulled out my warm-up suit and suggested I remove my shirt and tie. After I changed, Dan reminded me I hadn't eaten for a while, so he took me to a favorite restaurant for lunch. I ordered food but only picked at it. I felt completely removed from my surroundings. The buzz of conversation and laughter around me seemed like it was somewhere else. And how could people be in laughter on this day after everything that happened? It was surreal. Dan suggested we drive to Mt. Charleston to see the snow. He was continuing to be his sensitive and caring self. We walked along a stone sidewalk. The mountains glistened white and my attempts to focus on the striking beauty of the landscape pulled me back into reality.

While there are many kinds of trauma that may drive a person to dissociate—and many ways in which one might de-personalize—I have noticed a common phenomenon. Dissociative experiences, regardless of how they occur–trauma, deep meditation, etc.–can lead to changes in the way we experience consciousness. This change has the potential to cause our perceptions to pierce the veil between this dimension and the next. The information-carrying energy body that becomes the facilitator of this process is our activated torsion field. Individuals who dissociate often find themselves afterward experiencing a keener perceptual ability or even extra sensory perception.

Katherine was a home health nurse. When she arrived at the home of a patient, unexpectedly she found an upsetting and chaotic suicide scene. Nonetheless, she supported family members at taking care of business. She and her coworker notified case management personnel, the coroner, and her patient's relatives. They also helped clean up the scene. When her workday was over and she was returning to her home, she felt a hot flash and realized that her left arm had become numb. There was no feeling and thank goodness she drove skillfully with her right hand. Such symptoms relate to an experience called conversion disorder–the traumatic experience is somehow converted into a physical symptom. Fortunately, by the time she reached her home, Katherine's left arm was alive again.

Members of the first responders therapy group that Katherine subsequently attended expressed compassion and understanding as she described her experience. As I helped Katherine with processing her feelings I had no idea that her emotional disclosures would have a contagious effect on the group.

As the group offered Katherine their heartfelt empathy, two other group members began experiencing unprocessed traumatic memories. They empathized with Katherine so exquisitely that their own traumatic experiences flooded back. I was doing my best to facilitate three individuals in group who were having flashbacks and dissociating all at the same time. Running on pure intuition, I pulled interventions seemingly out of the air and we all got through it, one at a time. Before the group was concluded, all individuals had accomplished some processing and had come back to reality. With any triggers or traumatic events that may occur, whole groups of people may be in dissociative symptoms all at the same time. Torsion fields amplify and individuals will talk of perceptions becoming finely tuned both during and after a traumatic event. Kathrine testified to that.

Occasionally I have been called upon to facilitate critical incident stress debriefings. When individuals experience an on-the-job trauma I will conduct a debriefing session for them in the hopes of averting full-blown post-traumatic stress. Late one afternoon an insurance company called me in to help manage the emotions of bank employees after a robbery.

Robert was the most traumatized employee. A thief stood directly in front of him pointing a gun at his face. As Robert removed the cash from the drawer his body grew numb. His perception of the gunman shrank in size and he appeared to be small and far away. As Robert dissociated, he thought of his parents: "If I die today I won't be there to take care of them." When his drawer was empty, not being able to speak, Robert held up both hands and wiggled them indicating there was no more. The gunman took the cash and ran. Robert sank to the floor where he sat in shocked stillness for several moments. I was called to the scene shortly thereafter and began my debriefing procedure. Once I understood that Robert experienced the worst stress of all, I invited him to attend individual therapy. When he went back to work the next week, he explained, "My perceptions are entirely changed. I feel that I can see into people now! I know who they are when I look at them, and that's new for me."

As I occasionally engage in a bit of dream work with my patients when requested, I find that many individuals experience prophetic dreams. This indicates to me that my theory of the torsion field conveying information from the next dimension to the place where our consciousness lives makes sense. After 9-11, individuals around the world indicated that they had a pre-cognitive dream about such an event. One of my friends remarked at the time, "The veil between this dimension and the next is getting thinner." Perhaps, but I have an additional theory. Secondary trauma is what happens when we observe or hear about the discomfort and suffering of others. When they tell their story, our mind sees it in animated images and we develop feelings about their experience. Knowing that others have suffered hurts, we can develop various levels of dissociation from seeing something frightening happen to them, as well as experiencing it personally. What if society itself has developed a thin layer of dissociation due to increasing awareness of trauma as it appears around us? When I was a child, images of war came to us in news reels that we saw in movie theaters only once in a while, and they were censored to minimize violent images. But improvements in technology such as advanced video photography brought images of the Vietnam War literally into our living room. Censorship of violent images shown to the public has eroded over the years.

On September 11, 2001 I was walking through the grocery store when I saw shoppers and employees gathered around a television at the front of the store. New Yorkers on the screen were screaming as planes flew into buildings and people ran for their lives. My favorite clerk looked at me with teary eyes and fear in her face. "Oh my God," she said. "What's going on?" Millions of Americans had those same feelings on that day.

That was a sudden traumatic event that happened years ago. But even as I write there are things happening in our country that are troubling for many of us. Confidence in our national leaders is at an all-time low. Thanks to instant communication, their lies, manipulations, and personal wealth-creating schemes at the expense of the population are constantly exposed. Economic breakdown is evident with wealth flowing like a river to the people at the very top. We probably all know someone who lost a home to foreclosure. Our country is involved in perpetual war on other continents leaving chaos behind after our troops have left, not to mention the trauma actually experienced by the soldiers. And in spite of healthcare changes, up to this point we are dealing with a miserably flawed healthcare system. In my opinion, all of these things add to the traumatic effect on society and contribute to feelings of tremendous vulnerability. We vacillate between desensitization to what's happening and traumatization, which contributes to dissociation at a societal level.

We experience the next dimension more frequently as the veil between this dimension and the next grows thinner.

Figure 1 below indicates some of the subject matter that I've discussed so far:

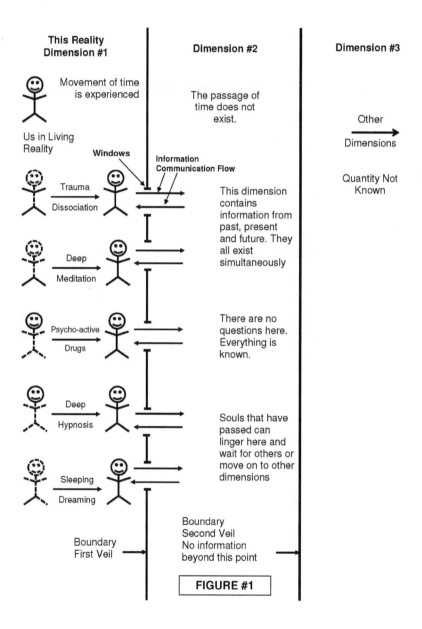

FIGURE #1

It's important to remember, when discussing changes in perception as a result of dissociation and depersonalization, that the nature of an individual's perceptions is contingent upon the state of consciousness they're in when that perception takes place, as well as the brain wave patterns they are experiencing.

My friend, Ilene, lost her husband after many years of a good marriage and giving birth to several children who were now grown and independent. One afternoon, after her husband's death, Ilene dozed on the living room sofa. She was just rousing from sleep when she looked over at her husband's favorite chair. He was sitting there comfortably looking directly at her. As their gaze met he told her, "Don't worry about me, I'm okay." Then he disappeared. When Ilene told her story I realized that I had heard several other such stories that were identical to hers. Science claims that such experiences are a brief, reactive psychosis. I say not always. I believe that a dissociative state combined with a state of consciousness with specific brain waves can provide a window between dimensions. These experiences frequently happen between waking and sleeping, and they are organized, specific communications, not dreams. I believe these experiences to be visions of a spiritual nature. Did Ilene's husband disappear or did she just wake up a little more, change her state of consciousness from theta brain waves to alpha, and lose contact with him?

Figure 2 illustrates the place on the brain wave spectrum that reflects a psychic window. The significant moment in the brain wave pattern starts with light sleep—theta–and proceeds into the lower part of theta brain waves:

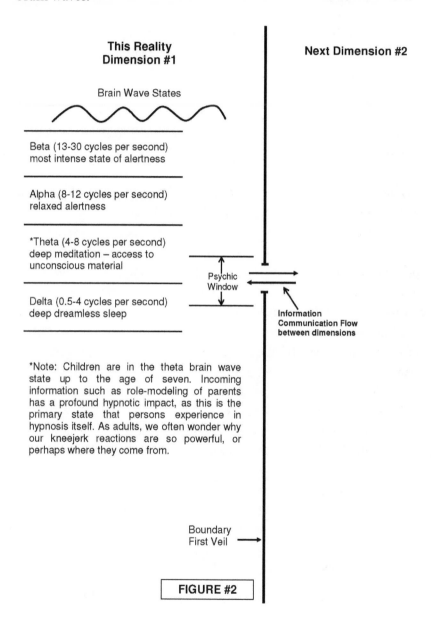

**This Reality
Dimension #1**

Next Dimension #2

Brain Wave States

Beta (13-30 cycles per second)
most intense state of alertness

Alpha (8-12 cycles per second)
relaxed alertness

*Theta (4-8 cycles per second)
deep meditation – access to
unconscious material

Psychic
Window

Delta (0.5-4 cycles per second)
deep dreamless sleep

Information
Communication Flow
between dimensions

*Note: Children are in the theta brain wave state up to the age of seven. Incoming information such as role-modeling of parents has a profound hypnotic impact, as this is the primary state that persons experience in hypnosis itself. As adults, we often wonder why our kneejerk reactions are so powerful, or perhaps where they come from.

Boundary
First Veil ⟶

FIGURE #2

While watching a true psychic or spiritual medium at work, you will notice them pass into a trance-like state which is an intuitional way of finding the window in the veil that enables them to glean information from the next dimension.

So what about the next dimension? How is it conceptualized? What is beyond the border which separates our DNA-based three-dimensional reality from a dimension that seems to be of the spirit? In this case, I can only refer to the amazing testimonials given to me by my patients and friends. There is an uncanny congruence and uniformity in these stories. Even though this is not science, I can turn to science to create a metaphor.

We live in a three-dimensional physical reality. We see length, breadth, and depth. Recently, I watched an interesting video where theoretical physicist, Dr. Michio Kaku, discussed the possibility of other dimensions.[13] He and many other scientists now believe that this is possible. In his presentation, Kaku cited the example of a fish whose eyes are on the side of its head, which prevents it from seeing in front. For this fish, there is no *up*. Kaku asks, "What if the fish living in this two-dimensional world were a scientist? If I grabbed him and lifted him *up*, he would see things in our three-dimensional world that he doesn't see in his own. He would see beings breathing without water." This metaphor translates to us, living in a three-dimensional world in which we occasionally dissociate (experience the *up*), getting a glimpse into a dimension that exists beyond our physical reality, just like the fish does when it's lifted from its two-dimensional reality.

Below are common characteristics of the next dimension as they have been related to me by patients and friends who have been lifted *up* through dissociative experiences:

A. Time does not exist.

B. It's the first place the spirit/consciousness goes when we die.

C. There are no questions there. If a curious thought comes to mind while our consciousness inhabits the next dimension, the answer is known immediately. Theosophists refer to the source of this knowing as the Akashic records. The Akashic records are described as "a compendium of thoughts, events and emotions believed by theosophists to be encoded in a non-physical plane of existence known as the astral plane."[14] There are anecdotal accounts, but no scientific evidence for the existence of the Akashic records. Dissociative clients have described this phenomenon without knowing that there's a name for it and theosophical writings that describe it.

D. Information from the past, present and future exist simultaneously.

E. Spirits of people who have died may be there.

But I feel that there is still one more variable in communication between our reality and the next dimension. What if the message coming from this dimension is urgent? Might it then circumvent all of the common variables such as dissociation and brain wave qualities? I believe so. Telepathic messages are a reality. I believe we have the ability to transmit and receive messages from others through the torsion field. The one constant in such telepathic situations is the intensity of the feelings of participants.

Perry, a skilled physician, described his own story of telepathy and an urgent message in an emergency situation. Perry went about his work with devotion and compassion for other people's lives. But so far as spiritual or religious beliefs, he had none. His face turned red if I mentioned religion which he believed "caused more problems in the world than you could have in all your imaginings!"

One busy afternoon Perry was working diligently miles away from his home. Suddenly, an image of his wife came into his consciousness. She had a look of hurt on her face and there were blurry details around her indicating a chaotic environment. "Something's really wrong," he thought. This was long before the days of cell phones. He took a break and began calling neighbors. One of them informed him that at the exact time the image came into his thoughts, his wife was in a serious automobile accident and was hospitalized. "We were just going to call you," they said. Sitting at his wife's bedside later, Perry tried to understand his telepathic experience. "I'll never forget it," he told me. "That was the day I learned that there's more to human existence than we can see, feel, and touch." When Perry's wife had her traumatic moment, according to my theory, her torsion field activated. She called out to him and he received her message. In their life together, they lived in spiritual connection.

There are many factors that can make telepathic communication possible. When one dissociates, an increased sensitivity occurs and a spiritual or energy-based opening is created in one's consciousness facilitating telepathic communication. There may also be situational factors that create heightened emotions that make reaching out to others more of a possibility.

I referred my friend, John to one of my peers for psychotherapy in order that he could deal with some traumatic experiences that occurred in his childhood. It was always clear to me that he was a person who had many dissociative experiences including out-of-body. I always wondered if dissociative tendencies increased the possibility of telepathic abilities and experiences.

In his life of healing, camping was one of John's favorite pastimes. On one particular evening, it was time to leave the campsite in the forest and get back to the city. Other friends had assisted with cleanup and left John as the last one to leave. When he reached his truck, however it would not start as the battery was suddenly dead. At this point in time cell phone reception was limited. John was stuck in the forest until morning when he would attempt to walk and find a forest ranger. His thoughts were of our friend, Roger, who was the last one to leave the campsite before John. John thought, "If only he had waited.................."

An hour passed, and as John sat quietly in his truck preparing for an uncomfortable sleep, he saw two headlights unexpectedly coming his way. It was Roger who proclaimed, "I got halfway home and felt that something wasn't right with you. When I couldn't reach your cell phone I turned around to make sure you had left safely." So...........did Roger hear our friend's silent telepathic call? This was beyond coincidence!"

What happened to Perry and John can be referred to as thought broadcasting. In the mental health profession, belief in such things is considered a psychotic symptom. If I were to express to "some" of my colleagues the belief that this phenomenon could be real, I might be shamed and marginalized. In some states my license to practice might be questioned. Hopefully a day will come when it's realized that within our reality both psychosis and clairvoyance are part of the human experience. Not everyone that hears a voice or experiences an internal message is mentally ill.

* * *

THREE

"The most beautiful thing we can experience is the mysterious." Albert Einstein

Out of Body, Into Spirit

Several years ago I attended the National Minority AIDS Conference in Palm Springs, California to improve my therapeutic skills in counseling HIV-positive patients and persons who had endured trauma. The day after the conference ended, as I lay in bed thinking about driving back home to Las Vegas, I was relaxed and not quite asleep with my eyes closed. Suddenly, *whoosh!* I was floating out of my body up toward the beamed ceiling of the bedroom. I was confused when I looked down and saw my body small and far away in the hotel bed. But then I was excited as my internal voice said, "Wow! That's me!" I was seeing my white t-shirt. In a second or two I returned to my body, opened my eyes and took a deep breath. I realized that I had an out-of-body experience—but why? This experience did not fit into my theoretical models. Perhaps it happened because I had been overwhelmed with information about HIV for three days, which raised my own buried grief with having lost two-hundred patients in our agency to HIV. Perhaps it happened because I realized I would soon lose my dear friend, David, who lived in Palm Springs, to HIV disease.

I didn't return to Palm Springs for a long time. David died and it was difficult for me not to see him, to no longer enjoy his warmth and dry humor. I associated Palm Springs with losing David. It wasn't until a great opportunity for more continuing therapeutic education arose that I went back to Palm Springs for a conference.

On the morning I was scheduled to drive back to Las Vegas, just as it happened before, I lay in my bed comfortably between waking and sleeping when, *whoosh!* I was out-of-body again. This time I was neither confused nor surprised. I knew what I was experiencing and stayed calm. My consciousness was out by the pool and beautiful grounds of the hotel. I could see in every direction. Suddenly, I saw a male figure, dressed in black and hooded, walking beside the pool and away from my vantage point. I understood this figure was a traditional symbol of death, and my internal voice said, "Yes, I understand. There's been a great many deaths here." I was referring to all the gay men, including my friend, David, who had died of AIDS in Palm Springs. Once that thought flashed through my mind I was back in my body.

I pondered this experience as I drove home. While having breakfast with my mother the next day the president of our agency's Board of Directors called. He was quite upset and told me that our Vice President was found dead in his car two nights before. It was clear to me that a symbol of death had stopped by my Palm Springs hotel to give me a message.

So, how do we deal with out-of-body experiences when they appear in psychotherapy? We validate them. There are certain phenomena that must be confronted or questioned in therapy, but not this one. If the experience is real to a patient, it matters. Unfortunately, in the past, patients having out-of-body experiences have been diagnosed delusional or hallucinatory and often prescribed harmful medication. Many clinicians who haven't been properly schooled in trauma therapy have left their patients confused with unanswered questions. These people have never felt their psychotherapy was complete or effective. But in recognizing my own experiences as well as those of friends and patients, I've been able to integrate understanding and validation of out-of-body episodes into more effective treatment.

James, who worked as a mechanic, had innocently entered a bank to conduct business. While he was there a group of armed thugs charged in the front door and demanded cash from the tellers. "Hit the floor," the robbers screamed and James obediently remained frozen in place. When the hoodlums were leaving with the cash, James lunged forward and tripped the last thief who was on his way out. One of the other perpetrators turned around and shot James three times.

When he came to me for therapy, he said, "I have no idea how you can help me." His symptoms were a textbook example of post-traumatic stress including nightmares, flashbacks, and a constant sense of looming danger. The thought of going into a bank was scary. James and I examined his perceptions and feelings through a technique called Prolonged Exposure Therapy which involves recounting events and accessing the associated feelings in order that the emotions begin to subside. By the fourth session I was concerned that James seemed to be "stuck" and had relinquished only part of his symptoms. I had my own hypothesis about what was happening and took a risk. "So tell me," I asked. "At what point did you leave your body?" James' face turned red and his eyes grew big as saucers and filled with tears.

"I can talk about that?" he asked. "You won't think I'm crazy?"

I nodded with encouragement and he continued.

"It was when I arrived in the emergency room," James remembered. "I thought for sure that my life was over and I was in the jumping-off place. But I made it by the skin of my teeth. When I was in the ER I kept going in and out of my body. One minute I'd be up on the ceiling watching them work on me, trying to stop the bleeding. In the next minute, I'd be back in my body with all kinds of terrifying feelings and pain." We explored all of James' feelings in depth and I was aware that we had passed a milestone as he physically and emotionally relaxed after those disclosures. I was convinced when he described the bank robbery and being shot that James had gone out-of-body, so how could I not have asked the question and how could we not have talked about it? I've asked that question a time or two only to see a feeling of relief on the face of a traumatized person.

Randy's out-of-body experience was different because he indeed penetrated the veil between this dimension and the next. He was a war veteran and worked as an investment counselor. He had a happy marriage and grown children with successful lives. His demeanor was youthful and he had a strong frame. When I assessed him to determine his therapeutic needs, he said, "I'm not done with the war. I've been in therapy groups and talked with a couple people alone and there are still things I don't understand. I have questions. People either didn't understand me or looked at me as though I'm crazy." Randy had been through extensive treatment for post-traumatic stress, but there were still areas untouched, and my intuition told me not to push. I allowed our times together to unfold.

We first talked about dreams. Randy said that most of his nightmares had subsided, and his dreams were now filled with repetitive images that had appeared in his dream life while he was at war. There were images of tall pine trees and stone walkways as seen in the state parks that he visited with his parents as a child. They were far from unpleasant, just repetitive. Images of fishing in streams and lakes recurred. Randy explained, "They're not scary. It's the constant repetition that makes me think they mean something." We took some of the common dreams and broke them down into smaller parts to examine the symbols and images. More important, we looked at his feelings.

Randy was only nineteen when he became a soldier and his days at war in a desert environment were terrifying. The underlying theme of the recurring dream images he described was really his intense longing for the life he left in Michigan. "Sounds like images of home," I said. "And home was a wonderful, safe place."

"Yes!" he said, as though he was talking through time as his younger self who was scared and at war. "I want to go home! Just take me home! All those beautiful things are there!" The fact that he was home now had not connected with the deep unconscious desire that was embedded in his memories of when he was in combat. In some ways, he was frozen in the thoughts he experienced there. I encouraged Randy to actually do the things he dreamed about—go to some state parks and have some fun; take a fishing trip and immerse himself in the safe situation he dreamed about with the intention, "I AM home!" It needed to be a "felt" experience. This was the release Randy very much needed. It all made sense. During our next session, Randy looked as though a weight had been lifted from his shoulders.

However, Randy explained, "There's one more thing. I tried to talk about this at the other treatment center but no one could explain it or help me. They looked at me like I was crazy." I encouraged Randy to take his time and pay attention to the details in his memory. What we found in the "one more thing" was actually very big.

"We were in the midst of enemy soldiers as they surrounded our position," Randy recalled. "I was on the top of a slight grade with my fellow soldiers in a fairly open area. After all, it was the desert. There were enemy behind us and also some at a distance in front of us. I knew that there were ten of them for every one of us. We decided to move down the hill to the front. I was afraid that I would die there. I didn't see a way that I could come out of it alive. We continued to move down the grade, but enemy gunfire was all around. But all of a sudden I could see myself and everyone else from above, and I was watching me as I fired my rifle. But somehow, from this weird perspective, I could see a glow around the bodies of some of the men that were further down the grade. It still haunts me from time to time when I'm awake, but especially in my dreams. The ones who had a glow around them are the ones who died. I couldn't save them. Why couldn't I save them?"

I explained that I believed Randy had dissociated out of sheer terror. His consciousness flew out-of-body. His torsion field was charged and brought Randy into contact with a window into the next dimension. While in that place, he was given specific information about who would be lost.

"How was I given special information about life and death?" he asked.

"Because in your trauma," I said, "you had a spiritual experience and for a moment, your consciousness pierced the veil between this dimension and the next. And on the other side of that veil all information about past, present and future exists simultaneously. You looked into moments in the future that really weren't very far away." I'd heard this story from veterans so many times.

Randy understood and the fuzzy images he'd carried for years became clear with less intense emotions as we went through the process of psychotherapy. What he needed was some explanation. We spent a couple more sessions on current issues and then I discharged him. The next time I saw Randy, he was coincidentally standing at a war memorial when I just happened to be visiting in Washington. It was a powerful moment of synchronicity.

"I didn't know these feelings would still be so big," he said as he looked over at me with great surprise as I stood beside him. "But I can feel them now and it means I'm okay." I believe Randy fully understands his spiritual experience. I'm sure that he will continue to make meaning of it as he travels through time.

Marty, however, had a different story. At the age of nineteen, his experience also happened during his service in Middle East. When he came to me for treatment for post-traumatic stress I realized that his condition was raw and untreated. We had a great deal of work to do. He described his time out in the field as emotional whiplash. "It all went by so fast," he said. "I didn't have time to think and put things in order in my mind." His remarks made sense because in post-traumatic stress the frontal lobes of the brain decrease in activity and placing experiences in order becomes difficult.

Just as I had with James, I began treatment of Marty with Prolonged Exposure Therapy. We took time to clarify events and situations. As Marty recalled traumatic incidents, we carefully examined the events and his feelings about them. Sometimes we went over the same scenario twice or three times until the intensity of Marty's emotions diminished significantly.

As we neared what I thought would be the end of his treatment, Marty looked at me with deep concern. He had saved this conversation until we'd built enough trust in our therapeutic relationship. "Promise you won't think I'm crazy?" he asked.

"Well, I haven't so far," I said, "So the chances aren't very likely."

"I had wondered away from the other guys thinking that they were still close by. After I went behind some rocks, I felt someone grab me from behind. I became paralyzed with fear because I thought they would kill me. I literally peed my pants! They were speaking in their own language and bound my wrists tightly with rope and held me there. They banged on my body. Nightfall came and I was terrified and in pain." As he remembered this incident Marty's demeanor changed. Tiny beads of perspiration appeared on his forehead, his hands trembled, and he began taking shorter breaths. I was afraid he would go into complete hyperventilation, but I encouraged him to continue the story.

"Of course everyone knew I was missing and they were obviously looking for me," he said. "When morning came my fellow soldiers found me and what commenced was a chaotic struggle with gun fire. Certain I would be caught in the crossfire and possibly killed, I went numb and started seeing everything from above including my own body that was bound with rope. As one of my captors was shot, I saw a shocking thing. I saw his spirit leave his body and travel upward and disappear. Then I was rescued and taken back to my company. My wrists were bleeding and my body hurt in places where I was punched and kicked."

Then Marty held up his wrists and displayed red welts that formed rings right below his hands. These welts had appeared during our emotional discussion. He explained, "I often get up in the morning like this after the dreams." While the welts always eventually vanished, it was apparent Marty was experiencing a phenomenon known as "body memories." This is what happens when a traumatic memory is so powerful that the place where the body was affected displays something symptomatic and physical. The other obvious phenomenon described in his story is that Marty dissociated and gained a precise view of life and death as he witnessed one of his captor's spirit leave the body.

I explained his dissociative experience and prepared for what would be the last part of treatment. I invited Marty to come in on a Saturday when the office was empty. When he went into a memory of the time in captivity, I asked him to make whatever sounds with his voice that he failed to make when he was in and out of dissociative states. At first, he closed his eyes and mumbled and groaned. Then it was as if his entire body had become electrified, as though he somehow snapped. He finally did what he needed to do for years as he closed his eyes tightly, went into the image of the experience, and screamed. Then he screamed some more. His body formed into the position he would have been in while being held in captivity. He had that limp, "wrung-out" look when we finished and his tears flowed freely. Breathing deeply, in a soft voice he said, "Wow! I really did need that!"

Marty returned the following Saturday. He explained that he went home and slept for two hours after our last session, and then he stated emphatically, "And I'm okay!" His nightmares were gone and there were no more welts on his wrists in the morning. Knowing that he experienced dissociation, I asked Marty if he noticed any changes in any part of himself in a "before and after" context.

"When I walk into a room full of people," he said, "I can feel who they are, and my wife says I'm BACK! I'm alive again!" That was the last time I saw him.

While most dissociative experiences are the result of traumatic experience, there are some who can produce these experiences at will.

I had just finished a course of growth-oriented psychotherapy with Richard. He was a self-made person who rose through the ranks in the retail industry. As a gay man, he valued his relationship with a long-term partner and cared deeply for his extended family. We were getting to the end of the assistance that he needed from me when we journeyed to a very different place.

"I have a question that's completely off the subjects we've discussed," he said. "Do you believe in dreams?"

"Of course," I said. "They're the mirrors of our unconscious mind and can reflect experiences we've had. Tell me about yours."

"They're very strange and I don't understand them," Richard said. "Right before I fall asleep, it's like something clicks or snaps and I find myself in various environments. Some of them are familiar and are places I've been. Some of them are new and unfamiliar. But I get scared. I'm there in these places, but my body isn't. In fact, I get scared because I don't know where my body is."

Richard's confusion was typical of someone having out-of-body experiences–or who is engaged in remote viewing ("psych-seeing" of faraway places)–but who has not yet developed an understanding of the phenomenon. Once I explained the experience to him, Richard agreed that this was what was happening. It was rather fun to watch him educate himself and to understand that he could be out-of-body at will.

As his understanding of his experience deepened, Richard's intuition dramatically increased. He developed "senses" about events and people around him. They were usually quite accurate. One big prediction haunting him since he understood his gift is a sense that something huge is going to happen that will change the way we live on earth. It will be extremely positive and dissolve the usurious powers and people that feed off other members of humanity, although he is not able to clarify beyond that feeling. For Richard, the out-of-body experience has been a positive and growth-filled function of his own consciousness and spirit.

Sharing time with these enlightened individuals is a privilege. I can conclude such therapy sessions with a sense that I am awakening to a new reality that validates my faith in the process of healing and spiritual growth.

* * *

FOUR

"It is the power of the mind to be unconquerable." Seneca

Escape from Terror: The Power of Human Consciousness

When I was five years old I remember my family talking about "concentration camps." My grandmother had long conversations on the telephone in Polish, her native language. I didn't understand any of this until October 12, 1949 when my father came to collect me from kindergarten. As we drove to my grandparents' home he told me, "You're going to meet a very nice man and lady today." The woman was my mother's cousin, Mary Szymerski, and the man was her husband, Kasimir. My family had sponsored their emigration from the Watenstadt displaced persons camp in Ober Braunschweig, Germany to our home in Pittsburgh, Pennsylvania.

Mary had been arrested by the Nazis when they discovered she was part of the underground resistance. Her father, Kazimir Rydaroski, who owned a forging mill and machine shop, saved hundreds of lives by making his shop and family mansion a waystation for the Underground. Cousin Mary, whose Catholic faith inspired her to personal acts of charity and kindness, worked hard for the Underground. When she was identified by the Nazis, she was the first person in her village to be arrested as a political prisoner, and throughout the war was moved from concentration camp to concentration camp. Near the end of the war Mary was locked into a solitary starvation cell and left to die. In telling her story later, Mary remembered many people who gave up, who "pulled the covers over their heads and died." Mary's decision was the opposite: she understood that will and faith were essential to survival and she decided to fight for survival with every part of her being.

She accomplished this by willfully dissociating in two ways. Her first method was concentrating on prayer. She separated herself from the stark reality of her cell by praying and creating the imagery of her survival. During these times, she recalled, a benefactor whose identity she never learned, tossed bread crusts at night through the bars of the small window in her cell. These crusts of bread kept Mary physically alive. I've often wondered whether, at this moment of great crisis in her life, Mary's torsion field activated with the emotions of deep desire and reached someone who responded with compassion and an effort to help her.

The second way Mary survived was through a self-induced "trance" during which she traveled to a safe place in her consciousness. Mary was an excellent seamstress with great pride in her work. In these moments of trance, Mary traveled to an imaginary world that epitomized her future survival. She visited a fabric merchant, chose cloth and patterns, and hand-stitched beautiful dresses in her mind. This willful dissociation occurred while she endured the cold and neglect of her starvation cell. Yet escaping into this imaginary world, doing something she loved with joy, was the imagery of survival to which she held tightly.

At the end of the war in April 1945 when the Nazis decided to execute all the prisoners they held, Mary was taken from her cell, stripped naked, given a towel, and told to go to the showers which were actually gas chambers. She stood naked in line with guards and guns behind her. But the line didn't move and no one went into the gas chamber. Sounds of chaos echoed from outside the camp. The British Army was storming the gates and this was Mary's day of freedom. She was eventually moved to Watenstadt, where she met Kasimir, was married, and immigrated to the United States. Years into her new life in America, Mary often presented women in the family with dolls that were wearing native Polish costumes she had sewn. This sewing was Mary's debriefing from the nightmare of her captivity. What she had imagined in her effort to survive manifested in her freedom and recovery.

The day I first met my cousin Mary she looked down at me and remarked, "*Jaki ladnychlopczyk*! You are a nice little boy," as my father served as interpreter. Later I realized that on that day I connected with the person who would give me my first lesson in the power of human consciousness. The great psychiatrist Victor Frankl said, "Everything can be taken from a man but one thing: the last of human freedoms – to choose one's attitude in any given set of circumstances, to choose one's own way." Mary did indeed choose her own way through empowering her own consciousness. When I was a teenager describing to Cousin Mary the car I wanted, she reminded me, "Material things can come and go, but what you cultivate in your own mind and your own heart no one can ever take away. You must cultivate those parts of you!"

Once I began facilitating psychotherapy—and with Cousin Mary in mind–I made certain I had a plan for helping my patients deal with emotional trauma:

1) **Educate the patient regarding the trauma recovery process**. Give your patient some idea about the treatment process and the intended end result.

2) **Create and/or define what constitutes a safe place** for your patient to tell their story. The office surroundings should be warm and welcoming. A comfortable atmosphere will help your patient trust you and the process.

3) **Help the patient create a calm, safe internal space.** It's been no surprise regarding the number of persons experiencing trauma who have never known a safe space. Would it be memories of a beach with gentle waves in the surf or Grandma's kitchen? Determine what would help your patient feel safe while relating their traumatic experiences.

4) **Telling the story.** What was it that happened as a traumatic event? I don't believe it necessary to put every detail on the

table. A general idea, however, of how the traumatic instance manifested is a good place to start.

5) **Assist your patient with methods of anxiety management.** Recalling traumatic memories can cause considerable anxiety. Offering a method to manage anxiety may be the tool that relieves the traumatized person from the cycle of symptoms, such as flashbacks. Guided imagery, breathing exercises, and mindful meditative techniques may be helpful.

6) **Engage therapeutic methods as traumatic memories present themselves.** Such treatment interventions as a general debriefing with both verbal descriptions and feelings that are actually "felt" can constitute a good beginning. Prolonged Exposure Therapy can take the patient more deeply into traumatic memories with feelings coming to the surface that will become far less intense once they are felt. A process called Eye Movement Desensitization Reprocessing can be extremely helpful. The psychotherapist assists the patient with creating the same conditions as rapid-eye movement sleep. Such actions can help access and de-intensify traumatic images and feelings. Hypnosis can help disarm environmental triggers that cause traumatic feelings to reappear. Additional interventions such as art therapy and journaling can also be very helpful. Cognitive Behavioral Therapy helps an individual to see the traumatic event through their own thoughts, behaviors, and interpretations as well as re-interpretation of events.

7) **Closure**–In this phase most of the intensities related to traumatic feelings have decreased in strength and dissipated. I find it's helpful for patients to make meaning-based statements about events that happened. Sometimes when I ask the question, "What does it mean to you that something like this happened?" I watch people struggle to answer. They are placed in a position to philosophize about their experience, which is a giant step past the trauma. It provides them opportunity to transcend and gain power over last vestiges of the trauma.

Many years later, the coping skills I recognized in my Cousin Mary were useful in treating Sabrina. When I welcomed Sabrina into my practice and asked her to explain her issues, her words shocked me.

"I was born in a concentration camp and my life has been fraught with images of terrorism and horror. I'm sixty-two years old and my husband says that I need help, so here I am. I've had doctors and psychiatrists all my life," she went on. "They give me pills that really don't help. I just don't know what to do. What do you know about people being in concentration camps?"

"Quite a bit," I responded. I described my cousin Mary and her husband. From that moment Sabrina trusted me and we moved on to her psychotherapy. At this point in time, I thought that everyone connected with the camps had passed away, as this was long after my cousin, Mary was gone. But Sabrina was born in one.

Like Mary, Sabrina's family was part of a Resistance movement. Their home was in Hungary. While her young mother was barely pregnant the Nazis had placed her parents on a train that headed right to a camp. Once there, Sabrina's father was part of a hard labor brigade and was separated from his wife and new-born child. Months after Sabrina was born, it was learned that her father had died along with other members of the work crew. Sabrina's mother worked to provide her child with as much nourishment as possible by food sharing in the place where they were housed. There were other mothers and children there as well and everyone corroborated as much as possible to make sure children were nourished. As months and then years passed Sabrina was placed in quarters with other children away from her mother. On rare occasions, her mother would sneak by to see her.

Everyone in the camps was brutalized, including the children. Women were raped by the guards. People who failed to perform work duties were beaten. Children were physically and sexually abused. As painful as it was for both of us, Sabrina and I did a debriefing of her experience and she faced her pain courageously and with feeling. I told her before we embarked on the telling of her story that, "We will keep one foot firmly planted in this reality and place the other foot in the other reality as needed for the purpose of healing." It's the treatment philosophy that I utilized with all of my traumatized patients.

Like so many survivors of trauma, Sabrina's consciousness and spirit came to her rescue. "When horrible things were happening," she said, "my spirit self would fly out into the fields outside the camp where it was lush with foliage, and the ponds were filled with water. The place was beautiful and I hung out there in mind and spirit over the reeds that were growing near the ponds." While she was in that beautiful place, Sabrina told me, she could not feel the pain of what was happening to her. "Then, at some point," she recalled, "What my body was experiencing was over. I would be back in my body and feeling terrible pain. I would cry myself to sleep and wonder if it would ever end. My mother kept telling me about the outside world and that we hoped to get back there, but this awful place was all I knew and I had trouble understanding what she was telling me. I learned to hide wherever I could so the guards would let me alone. I might have been about the same age that a child would be in the first grade. I knew no other world or any other kind of existence."

Sabrina's clinical profile was severe post-traumatic stress and she had a multitude of depressive symptoms. Physically, she had been diagnosed with severe fibromyalgia. She awoke screaming from nightmares. Elongated buildings served as emotional triggers and reminders of the camp and caused flashbacks. Electrical installations were another big trigger as they reminded her of the electrified fences in the camp where she watched anguished adults commit suicide by throwing themselves against the fences. In her adult years, with no forum to deal with her memories and emotions, Sabrina was glad to live in Las Vegas because she could escape her pain by trancing out in front of a gambling device. She spent her life expecting the worst possible things to occur, even though she was completely safe.

My biggest fear was that I would go too far into memories with Sabrina and traumatize her all over again. Like the others that I treated over the years, Sabrina was frozen in place by her trauma. If she moved forward into treatment she was afraid of drowning in an unstoppable torrent of emotions and images of horror. Yet refusing treatment would condemn her to physical and emotional suffering for the rest of her life.

In order to treat Sabrina, I had to move her out of her emotional stalemate. I created a visual metaphor for her on my white board. I drew a straight line and told Sabrina that it represented the surface of her life, like the surface of the earth. I erased part of the line and drew a hole in the imagined geography with a boulder beside it. I told her that all of her traumatic memories were stored there—but the hole had a bottom, and in time we would bring all those memories up to the surface. Sabrina herself could control how many memories she brought out of the hole by moving the boulder over it or away from it. If recollection grew too difficult, she could block the hole and then open it again when she felt safe and able to do so. The metaphor worked and our therapy proceeded at a pace Sabrina could best manage.

My experience treating Sabrina taught me not only how a person can become frozen in life through their inability to release traumatic memory, but clarified for me how their dissociative and spiritual experiences—such as what happened to my cousin Mary–helped them survive. I also learned about the concept of environmental and emotional triggers—how one little trigger, even just a few words, can bring traumatic memories forward like an emotional hurricane and cause a dissociative experience. As therapy came to a close, I'll never forget the day that she walked into my office and said, "Look at me!" The fibromyalgia symptoms had subsided and she moved her arms and shoulders back and forth as she was truly in the choreography of recovery. "And no more gambling!" she said proudly.

My patient, Mike, was a responsible adult and had grown into a talented man. He had graduated from college and worked as a computer programmer. He had come out as a gay man in his early twenties and his parents simply urged him to lead a good life, make good choices, and find warm companionship. But he had a great deal of trouble making connection with people, and felt both attraction and fear at the thought of anything physically or emotionally intimate. He was confused.

His family members were all practicing Catholics and took part in various Church activities. When Cardinal Ratzinger declared (before becoming Pope) that gay people were "intrinsically evil," Mike decided that he was done with the church, bowed out from all activities, and struggled to work through and author his own spiritual beliefs.

On one particular morning, however, a friend from his office was getting married and out of friendship for both the bride and groom, he decided to attend the church wedding. But somewhere in the middle of the service, Mike felt a tightness develop in his chest and he began perspiring profusely. What was this about? In therapy language and concepts, we call such experiences "affect bridges." It's about when feelings show themselves with no mental pictures to go with them. But the mental pictures eventually show up because the feelings that go with them have broken the amnesia and suppression. So Mike began having nightmares and a firm realization that he had been sexually abused by a priest in the church came flooding forward. That was the point at which Mike's anxiety spun out of control. He began having flashbacks, panic attacks, and more nightmares. This was when he came to me with his story.

When Mike was ten or eleven years old he was part of a religious instructions group that was facilitated by a priest. The cleric would often ask him to stay and "help" with chores after the group was over and this is when he began touching Mike. He cried, shook, and hyperventilated as he related his story. But soon it became far more than touching. Mike was scared and began to object. The priest reminded him that if he told anyone or objected too much, his whole family could end up going to hell. And this man was a "representative of God," wasn't he?

Because of the overwhelming nature of Mike's experience, I felt we needed a very rigorous recovery plan that would serve many functions. I also had to help Mike believe that his recovery was possible. I had learned through experience that psychotherapists don't need to dig into all the dark corners of someone's experience like voyeurs. After three sessions, I sent Mike home with an assignment to bring to session the worst experience that he could remember. That memory would symbolize all the other bad memories. I intended working at this memory with Prolonged Exposure Therapy to elicit emotions as well as descriptions of how his body and thoughts were affected by the experience. I also believed that since these memories lingered in amnesia for years, there was no way Mike could have had this experience without dissociating. I felt that looking for Mike's point of dissociation would help demystify his experience, clear confusion, and provide order to his chaotic memories. Knowing the beginning of his dissociative experience could also assist Mike with understanding that he had a built-in psycho-spiritual mechanism that protected him. First I had to give him some anxiety management skills. Mindfulness meditation served him well.

As Mike recalled the story about his worst experience of abuse he trembled and cried. When he began speaking in a little boy's voice describing the details of his most frightening memory, it was clear he had dissociated. What was being done to him was the source of great pain. Part of him was reliving the experience in flashback, but, of course, part of him was still in the office with me describing the experience. I reassured the part of Mike that was with me and for the first time he was able to disclose the full nature of his experience and how it affected him.

Suddenly, still in flashback, Mike described an amazing dissociative experience. "I wasn't in my body anymore," Mike said. "I was floating through the basement of the rectory, but my body was somewhere behind me with Father. 'No more pain. As I floated through, I could see all the stored equipment from the church fair that they had every year. There was gambling equipment because churches were allowed to do that. There were signs and what appeared to be food serving equipment." The dissociated embodiment of Mike's spiritual self, with the help of the torsion field, was transmitting information through "mind" that would store in his brain and be remembered. Like Sabrina, Mike found a way to move away from his pain. His out-of-body self wandered into an area where there was another room and—"I was able to pass right through the wall," he remembered. The tears Mike had been crying stopped all of a sudden.

Now, however, Mike's experience changed. "I'm scared!" he said. There's an opening like an archway in front me. It seems to be an opening to a hallway. Way down in this hallway I could see a very bright light, although it was very small like it was far away. But beside the archway there was a ghostly image of a woman. She was motioning with her hand and her index finger up. Her motions said, "No," referring to the archway. She was telling me not to go there.

I believe this to be a near-death experience, similar to what many others have described. As Mike's situation was so terrifying, could he have decided to give up and die, in the way my cousin Mary described others from her experience in the concentration camp? But Ghost Woman told Mike he could not go into the light because it was not his time. At this point Mike began weeping again. In the memory, he'd gone back into his body and was wracked with pain and fear. I assured Mike that he was safe now, in the present and that the pedophile abusing him was long gone and could no longer hurt him. He understood that being out of his body was a spiritual rescue from pain and fear. It was this reassurance in the moment of recollection that began Mike's healing.

While this abuse was occurring, Mike was able to escape the on-going experience thanks to a summer vacation at "Grandma's." He never went back to any religious instructions and these memories lodged themselves in amnesia until that morning at the wedding. Research told Mike that the priest was moved to another location and later arrested because the same thing had happened to others.

I've come to appreciate the importance of healing rituals for people who have experienced terrifying trauma. It's not just survivorship but transcendence to a life that's left the trauma behind. In concluding Mike's treatment, I utilized hypnosis to help deemphasize the traumatic memories and send them to a "quieter" place. As metaphor of strength, he chose the symbolism of Superman, and we decided that the part of him that could transcend this trauma had many of the characteristics of this folk hero; strong, unstoppable, powerful.

As part of the ritual, I suggested Mike find some symbol of Superman and his own survivorship. It would be a good idea to keep it in a meaningful place at home where he could see it. He followed my instruction explicitly. During the Christmas holiday several months later I found a loosely wrapped gift package stuffed into my office mailbox. Inside I found a small plastic statue of Superman. Attached to it was a note in large letters boldly stating, "MIKEY LIVES!"

What I learned from my Cousin Mary's stories of survival and transcendence, and from Sabrina and Mike's descriptions of the dissociative experiences that protected them, have not only provided me better tools for healing, but have given me some hope for the future. Mary chose her own way through a desperate situation by empowering her consciousness and visualizing her survival. Sabrina and Mike were saved by their natural ability to dissociate and send their consciousness to a safer place, away from pain. I often imagine what the possibilities might be if we all relied on our own tools of consciousness to resolve problems and disputes, and to advance our species rather than going to war.

* * *

FIVE

"The quality of your consciousness at this moment is what shapes the future." Eckhart Tolle

Psychics

The work of Edgar Cayce, renowned as the Sleeping Prophet, has always interested me. I believe he became a dissociative at an early age when he was in the woods with his grandfather and a bear attacked and killed the elder. It's my theory that Cayce dissociated at that terrifying moment and his consciousness found its way into the next dimension. Cayce told his family that his grandfather had communicated with him to say that he was okay and the family didn't need to worry. For the rest of his life Cayce made his predictions and provided past-life information and distance healing readings by dissociating into a deep trance where I believe he had access to information passed from another dimension.

When I was just out of high school my friend, Alice, introduced me to a psychic medium she'd met named Marlene Kaminski. There was nothing remarkable about Kaminski's appearance or the small house where she lived. "I'm just a plain old housewife," she said when we met. She could have been the woman next door in any neighborhood. While Alice waited on the sun porch Marlene led me into her kitchen where we sat at the table.

"Is there something that you have on you or with you most of time that I could use as a guide for your reading?" she asked. I removed my high school class ring and placed it in the middle of the table. "Perfect," she said. Staring at my ring, Marlene's gaze grew distant as she passed into an altered state of consciousness from which she could access the next dimension for information. She knew which of my grandparents were living and which were dead. She precisely named people who were close to me and noted a man in a Navy uniform who watched over me from the spirit world: this was my godfather, Thomas Gorazd, who had died in the Navy. "I can see you standing in the doorway of your home calling Rusty, Rusty. Who's Rusty?" Marlene asked. Rusty was my dog, and, at that time hardly a day went by when I didn't open the door and call him. Marlene told me that my true happiness would be "in the West." Many years later I left Pennsylvania for Las Vegas and recalled the prediction Marlene had made when I was still a young man. She also assured me I would "travel the world, many places, many times," a prediction I remembered decades later while I sat in an airport awaiting a flight to Poland. Much of what Marlene Kaminski told me was so accurate. I believe I was myself in an altered state of consciousness while she performed my reading which gave her further access to information from the next dimension. Marlene's use of my ring as her point of concentration suggests the subtle energy of our torsion field which hovers around objects we keep close and which carries information from the other side where past, present, and future exist simultaneously. The name for the process is psychometry.

There was no doubt in my mind that Marlene was the real thing, a true psychic who helped me understand at a young age that there was much more to our existence than what we can see or touch.

It was during my psychotherapy practice many years later that I met Susan, another person I consider to be a true psychic.

"I'm here to figure out what's going on with me," Susan informed as she sat comfortably in my office. When I examined her history, I learned that in the company of her family, she had been in a serious automobile accident as a child. A driver ran a red light and broadsided their vehicle on the driver's side. Susan had been in the back seat behind her father and was seriously hurt. She had lost consciousness at the time of the impact and was also unconscious for a day while in the hospital. "I've heard voices since that time," Susan related, "and there's a raft of other things going on as well.

Having grown into a young adult, Susan seemed to be well in charge of all of the other areas of her life. She was reliable on the job and produced quality work. She had years-long friendships with former schoolmates, and was active at all levels of family. People suffering from psychosis, which was my first suspicion when I learned that Susan heard voices, usually have major impairments in social and occupational functioning. That certainly wasn't her. We continued our appointments.

At the next meeting, I questioned her further about the voices. She explained she'd been hearing them from childhood from about a month after the accident until that present time. "Sometimes it's a man's voice and sometimes it's a woman's," she said. "They tell me something I need to know for the future, or maybe something that's about to happen. Sometimes it's not a voice, but an image or picture that I see, and it's about something that will happen soon. Sometimes it comes in a dream. When I watch the news I realize that the image I saw previously came true." She'd quit telling her fiancée, John, because it scared him.

When I asked for an example of her seeing some event before it happened, she described having seen a catastrophic air crash over water, and the next day heard and witnessed the news of the crash. "The only thing I can't understand," Susan told me, "Is the actual location where it's about to happen, and that's what's frustrating. I get really stressed and depressed. Who could I tell and what difference would it make? I don't know its location until I see it on the news."

Susan's story surprised me. I was expecting to see evidence of psychosis, but that was not the case. Voices that accompany schizophrenia usually have a critical or punitive quality, and they often criticize the patient or someone in his or her life. They are often violent in nature or suggest some violent act. But that's not what Susan described.

"There's another thing I need to tell you," she went on. "Do you believe in ghosts?"

"I might."

"We've got one in the house!" Susan said. Living with John, her fiancee, she related, "Sometimes at night it moves from room to room and I seem to know what it sees." This sounded like she was having an out-of-body experience. I asked her a leading question. "I wonder if that ghost could be you outside of your body?" Susan sat up, shocked.

"Oh my God," she said. "You're right! I just couldn't put it all together."

When I asked whether she'd ever been out of her body in the past, Susan went back to the time of the auto accident. "I was," she said, "But I didn't understand the experience until I started reflecting on it once I was physically well and almost grown up. I have distinct memories of floating above the car after the acident and seeing the emergency teams come to help me. I believe that my spirit was above the car, but my body was in it. Later on, in the hospital, I could see myself laying in the bed, then I woke up."

Susan told me that John and her parents knew about the predictive voices she heard and the images she witnessed. Constant out-of-body experiences and the qualities of her own consciousness had placed her in contact with the next dimension. Her torsion field energy was constantly active and picking up information expressed through psychic episodes. Because of the fears voiced by John and her parents Susan mostly kept her information to herself. Occasionally, however, the information she received was too important to go unsaid. She described attending a family gathering when news arrived that a cousin had had been in an constuction accident, fallen from a considerable height, and had died. The family's grief was extreme—but Susan saw images of her cousin alive, although gravely injured, which she announced to the family. Word came soon after that the cousin was indeed alive. He began regular breathing in the ambulance. "I was able to help my family settle down," Susan said. "When I could ease my family's pain, it felt good."

"Do you know what it means to be referred to as psychic?" I asked.

"It means people that can see the past and the future. I never understood that I was one of those people. But I guess that's what we're talking about, right?"

"Is this something you can accept?"

"Now that we're talking and it's clear; I guess so," Susan said.

She and I continued her treatment for some time. She had been traumatized from the accident as well as some past events which left issues she needed to resolve. But I also needed to help Susan accept and successfully manage her psychic abilities, and to bring her into clarity and full understanding of her life. It was as though I had a younger version of Marlene Kaminski sitting in front of me, and this part of her life was newly acknowledged. And I continued witnessing Susan's psychic episodes.

During one session when Susan developed a faraway look on her face I knew immediately that she had dissociated and that a momentary trance was present. "You're seeing something," I said. "What is it?"

"I'm sorry," she said. "You've had so much sadness. Someone close to you has died recently. I see him wearing blue jeans and his favorite shirts are plaid. He has a pair of brown lace-up shoes that he never wants to take off, and light brown hair. You were so close. Was he your partner?"

Susan had described my best friend, Jerry Chestnut, who had just died and my personal grief at his loss was still fresh. She said that Jerry was right beside me. "He's not moving on until he knows that you're okay." She would be the first person to relay such information, but not the last. "There was some conflict between the two of you," she went on. "He didn't think very much of himself sometimes, and you always argued that he was a good person. That's the part he holds close to him now in eternity."

All of this was true, down to the very last word. Susan continued. "And I see you on a beach with other people holding a banner that says goodbye. What was that about?"

"We interred his ashes out in the surf on his favorite beach," I said. I knew then that Susan was the real deal. Her confusion had lifted and it appeared that her psyche was metaphorically moving through time and space, past and future, straight as an arrow.

I continued working with Susan and helped her clarify some goals in regard to her upcoming marriage. John worked with an individual therapist for himself to facilitate some premarital counseling, and I left the door to the therapy room symbolically open in order that they could come in for tune-ups when necessary. As time passed, I saw Susan less frequently.

One particular day stands out. It was September 5, 2001 when she came to the front desk in our reception area asking to see me. She had no appointment, but was deeply distraught. Once we were settled in my office, she said, "They're very close."

"Who's very close?"

"The terrorists," she said. "It looks like a city is going to be bombed. I see a pile of rubble in a big city and there's people running everywhere. They're upset because they have trouble using their cell phones." Susan couldn't tell where this was going to happen and her frustration drove her to tears. There was no way she could warn anyone without specific information. Even if she could, she wondered if she would be believed. I made an appointment for her the following week on September 12th.

Susan had become part of the legion of individuals, worldwide, that were forewarned of the 9/11 tragedy through visions and dreams. Among the population of my own patients, she was not alone. Late that afternoon when I was home watching the terrorist attacks on television, I recognized Susan's vision in color on the big screen. The buildings had come down in a pile of rubble. A news reporter noted that rescue workers were having difficulty with poor or nonexistent cell phone reception. I had my own sense of shock at that moment, realizing Susan's prediction from just days ago had come true.

A few months later she sat on the sofa in my office, took a deep breath and said, "It's a school. I see kids being harmed. Lots of them. It's not here in this country. I'm thinking that it's somewhere in Europe. I just can't focus on the country." A few weeks later, in September 2004, Islamic militants from Chechnya attacked a school in Beslan, North Ossetia in Russia killing over 300 people, including 186 children. Susan's vision of drowning children in December 2004 manifested as the December 26 Indian Ocean earthquake and tsunami that killed more than 200,000 people in 14 countries.

Despite Susan's frustration and grief at being unable to more specifically identify the visions she experienced and her inability to warn of impending disaster, our continued therapy, as it occurred periodically, helped her develop more resilience. As she grew into her 30s, Susan became much more relaxed as a wife and mother and lived in full acceptance of her psychic abilities. She developed an enthusiasm for sharing her latest readings and insights and secretly helped others when she could. She offered the images and information passed to her from the other dimension as casual suggestions meant to assist others who had no knowledge or understanding of her gift. "I just try to keep my part of the world safe," she said. "I try to keep everyone around me healthy and strong."

At one point near the end of our therapeutic relationship, I benefited personally from Susan's talent when she noticed I was limping. "What's wrong?" she asked.

"I'm not sure. We just moved our household and I may have hurt myself."

Susan slipped into an altered state, then knelt in front of me and pulled up my right pant leg. She placed her hand on my right knee and closed her eyes for a moment. Looking up at me she explained, "You have a tear on the left side of your knee and you better get that fixed!" An MRI revealed I had a torn meniscus in that exact location.

I scheduled surgery.

Looking back on my experience of treating Susan, I hope I was as effective as I could be in improving her life, helping her past trauma and assisting her to reduce anxieties. It had also been a journey of self acceptance that helped her transform into a "knowing" woman of tremendous spiritual depth. Prior to then, I had never facilitated psychotherapy with a true psychic. She was the harbinger of others who would come. It was an honor sharing this experience with her. She's out in the world somewhere today, living as the silent, secret mystic, offering help to others with information that comes from her glimpses beyond the veil.

* * *

SIX

"Within a near-death experience, life changes, love grows and the universe moves into another world." Petra Hermans

The Empathic Near-Death Experience

The media is filled with stories about people who have had near-death experiences; individuals who die then return to life with memories of what happened to them in some place between life and death. These people commonly describe finding themselves at the mouth of, or traveling down a dark tunnel with a bright light at the end. Friends, loved ones, and even pets that have died are there to greet them in joyous reunion. They tell stories of places of unimaginable beauty, of feeling great ecstasy and joy. Many, however, reticent to return to physical life, are told they must go back, that they are needed "back there." Sometimes no reason is given but the order to return is clear, and the person who has "died" comes back into their physical body to continue living, bringing insight and spiritual change with them.

But the empathic near-death experience is different. This is a phenomenon experienced by the loved ones of those who are dying. Unlike the near-death experience itself, which has universal elements—a dark tunnel with a bright light, the presence of loved ones who have already passed over—the substance of an empathic near-death experience varies. It frequently includes specific dreams, visions, "ghostly" entities, disembodied voices, and familiar odors and fragrances. It's very individualized. While science too quickly calls such experiences delusions, hallucinations, or brief reactive psychoses, I believe that most of these experiences are trans-dimensional communicative phenomena carried through one's torsion field, and can be activated by the emotional and spiritual trauma of impending loss.

Those who study empathic near-death experience also note that the phenomenon is happening more frequently in the population. I believe this is because the population, in recent years across the world, has been traumatized by widespread economic failure, the violence of war and terrorism, the destruction of public trust, the collapse of our political institutions, and the spread of fear and insecurity. These have all combined to create trauma-related dissociation over our entire society. In turn, this makes contact with the next dimension much more possible and contributes to the frequency of dissociative phenomena and experiences such as precognitive dreams, extra-sensory perception, and striking visions of past, present and future, as well as awareness of deeply synchronistic events.

Likewise, as society becomes less religious it has become less susceptible to the controlling dogmas of organized religion, less influenced by opinionated notions of right and wrong, of "good" and "evil," and what constitutes moral or immoral behavior. Belief today is less dictated and limited and we hear many people profess, "I'm not religious, but I'm spiritual." And, of course, being spiritual by no means indicates that one can't have a morality. There's an openness to new experiences that occurs when religious dogma takes a back seat, and people are more likely to pay closer attention to experiences their religion once condemned and proscribed. The questioning of dogma and movement toward open-mindedness and latitude is the greatest spiritual gift a person can give themselves, which in turn, makes peering through the veil more possible. This all happens when we are no longer placing the symbolic footsteps of our lives over the imprints of others, and claiming our own power for spiritual authorship and belief.

As an inexperienced and slightly naïve therapist, I realized this rather quickly when working with AIDS patients who, in the early days of the epidemic, became terminally ill soon after diagnosis. I had walked into the hospital room of one of my patients and I can remember his mother clutching my arm as we stood at the bedside of her emaciated son.

"Oh my God," she exclaimed. "Look at what this terrible disease has done to my son's body!" I realized that she was traumatized and in shock. Her altered state, unencumbered by repressive religious dogma, was the conduit for her to have a spiritual experience with her dying son. Sitting quietly by his bedside she observed shadowy figures floating through the room as her son's life ebbed away. "I saw the ones who helped him on his journey," she said. In her state of quiet perception, her torsion field activated and she saw phenomena that might not have been visible to her in her every day, casual state of consciousness.

My good friend, Ilene, a hospice nurse, described an empathetic near-death experience she had with a patient that changed her attitude and perception.

"I was working with a dying patient and all my care-giving was completed, so I took the seat beside him and held his hand a bit," she said. "I projected love in his direction, wishing him peace for his journey. All of a sudden I realized that his chest had stopped moving and that he had taken his last breath. I was about to move out of my quiet state of consciousness and take care of business when I stopped in my tracks. As I looked over at his body, I saw this silvery cloud rise up above it and then continue moving upward. I was mesmerized and knew that I had just seen his soul leave his body. For me, this was huge. It didn't make me more religious, but instead assured me of our spiritual existence."

Something similar happened with a couple I once counseled. Steve and Linda were both dealing with the fact that Linda had cancer. Linda was experiencing stage four and was severely symptomatic. My initial work with them emphasized techniques Linda could practice to manage her pain as she did not want her last days with Steve lost in a stupor of pain killers.

As I continued therapy with the couple, Steve began showing signs of dissociation. As we talked, I watched him move into a "deer-in-the-headlights" stare. "This can't be happening," he told me. "I can't be losing her." An articulate and accomplished business man, Steve had been in control of almost everything around him. But his lack of control over Linda's impending death destabilized his own life and traumatized him. He could do little but remain quietly at Linda's bedside.

In our first meeting following Linda's death, Steve described the last moments of her life. "I saw her take that final shallow breath. Then her shimmering silvery spirit rose out of her body. And as that happened her spirit bent down and kissed me on the forehead! It was remarkable and loving. Then, feeling like I was in some other place, I watched her soul, in pure iridescent form, move upward and out of the room! I didn't believe in any such stuff," Steve went on, "But this changed me forever!" Steve himself was in a dissociated state of consciousness which assisted with viewing Linda's departure.

There are other ways one can have an empathic near-death experience that do not involve seeing a loved one's soul leave the body. A common phenomenon includes odors or fragrances associated with someone close who is dying. If the torsion field carries information, could fragrance be part of that? Perhaps a spiritual entity has come to help someone cross over and they are accompanied by an identifying fragrance. Or do they bring the odor specifically to us like a fragrant news flash that someone is about to die?

My mother remembers returning home from grocery shopping one afternoon and when she came into the house she was surrounded by the rich smell of roses. My father smelled nothing and my mother remembers the fragrance gradually dissipating. Not long after, my mother received a phone call from the U.S. Naval retirement home that her favorite uncle, John, had passed away about an hour before she had arrived at home. At the time she made no connection between the smell of roses and her Uncle John's death. Three days later when she walked into the funeral home to pay her last respects to Uncle John the fragrance of roses was profound. She suddenly realized the roses she had smelled at home the afternoon of Uncle John's death had been the message of his passing.

Another such olfactory empathic near-death experience happened to me during the emotionally charged days before my father died. As I was getting out of bed the day before he died I noted the fragrance of sweet flowers filling my bedroom. I couldn't identify it until my mother reminded me that her mother, my maternal grandmother, always wore a perfume called Lilies of the Valley. I realized then what the message was and knew my father's time was close. My grandmother had come to prepare me.

The most profound empathic near-death experience I had, however, involved my close friend, Jerry Chestnut.

Jerry was a case manager at our local HIV service organization. Since I was doing a great deal of psychotherapy at the time, with mutual patients, Jerry and I shared many phone conversations and strategized ways to assist them. We became best friends. Jerry had been in the Air Force and when he was released he moved to Las Vegas to live with his sister, Rebecca, and niece, Amber. He admitted to me that he had become infected with the HIV virus in the military.

My friendship with Jerry served a purpose more than companionship for me. It was a struggle for me to keep therapeutic boundaries between me and the AIDS patients I counseled because their needs were so great: groceries, housing, transportation, emotional and financial support. If I had not maintained therapeutic boundaries I could have lost myself in a bottomless pit while helping my patients with other survival needs. Maintaining these necessary therapeutic boundaries was also an emotional drain in a different way. But my friendship with Jerry Chestnut gave me the opportunity to be helpful and supportive outside a therapeutic context, which provided an emotional safety valve for me. Our relationship was good for him and for me as well.

During the time we had together Jerry and I traveled to Los Angeles and Santa Barbara, shared dinners and days and confided in one another. Jerry was tremendously independent. He refused some of the HIV medications popular during the early nineties because of their terrible side effects. "My choice," he said, "Is quality of life versus long life!" I had to respect that. During a visit to Venice Beach one unusually cold and windy day, Jerry spent time walking barefoot in the surf. When he returned to the boardwalk where I waited for him, concerned about what effect the wind and cold water might have on his weakened immune system, he said, "You look so worried, as if you're afraid I'm going to go out into the cold air, catch pneumonia and die. Well I'm already sick and I'm definitely going to die. So save yourself the energy of fretting and just hang out!" During one serious downturn in his health I had him admitted to our county hospital, where they were doing a wonderful job in caring for HIV patients. Jerry made it quite clear that he did not like hospitals, so when I went to bring him home he announced dramatically, "No more hospitals. Understand?"

The time of our friendship passed too quickly, and in the absence of today's effective HIV medications, he became increasingly ill. His sister and her husband had moved back to Indiana leaving his young niece, Amber, and I as his care givers. We engaged hospice and did all we could to make Jerry's last days comfortable.

During his final days Jerry spoke often about separating from his body. "I leave my body and go over and hang out in the corner of the room," he told me. "I look back at me for a while. Then, I drift back to my body and feel the pain again." We had long conversations about his experience and what it meant. In his clear moments he reminded me that he was indeed dying, but that after his death he didn't plan leaving spiritually until he knew I was okay. He intended to "hang around" until then.

By the middle of April 1994 Jerry was no longer able to communicate with me and was mostly out of consciousness. There was no doubt in my mind, however, that he knew when I was there. Over the last few days of Jerry's life Amber and I relieved one another as we cared for him. I had to maintain my work and professional obligations, while Amber had classes at the community college. I was torn by my own process of loss and the anguish I felt that Jerry was so deeply ill and dying. I wanted his suffering to end, but I also wanted the healthy Jerry back again.

Thursday, April 14, 1994 was a long and difficult day. In between my appointments and Amber's classes, we sat with Jerry. When the hospice nurse arrived to check his vital signs and his medication supplies she said she felt he would be gone within a few days. Later that night as I left Jerry's apartment and walked to my car, I felt someone touch me, as though I was being stroked softly with a feather. It was a profound experience and I stopped in my tracks. I was exhausted and drained, but made a mental note of what I felt and went home, remembering what Jerry had told me of his out-of-body journeys when he would "hang out" in the corner of his bedroom, and that he intended to hang around after he died to make sure I was all right.

Once I crawled into bed that night I was out cold. But about 2:00 a.m., I felt I had to go to the bathroom. Ordinarily I would have gotten up and gone—but this time I lay there between waking and sleeping. My eyes weren't yet open. Suddenly, I felt my spirit rise up from my body until I reached that critical place in consciousness where I could see through the veil into the next dimension. It's as though there was a hinge in the center of my body and my consciousness rose upward. My torsion field had activated. To my left I saw my bedroom, the nightlight, pictures on the wall. But what I saw to my right was astounding. Elevated off the floor was a silvery figure. Its head was round with no visible features. Its silvery body materialized downward from the head where it had form at the shoulders but was inexact at the bottom. There was an arch around the figure, dark inside, so that the silver figure itself stood out clearly. Bursts of light danced around the periphery of the arch. I felt unconditional love and understood that Jerry's spirit had followed me home. The message I received from the figure was something like, "I'm becoming THIS and you're worried? Settle down and be at peace!"

The last weekend of Jerry's life was painful as he fought to separate from his body. It was Monday morning, April 18, 1994 at 11:00 a. m. when the hospice nurse called me. "It's time for you to be here," she said. When I arrived at the apartment Jerry had taken his last breath and made his final separation.

Taken altogether, empathic near-death events such as the image of departing souls that Ilene and Steve described, the shadowy figures of emissaries from the other side who guide the loved onward, the specific fragrances and odors associated with the imminent death of a loved one, and the experiences I had preceding Jerry's death suggest that we have a spiritual body and that those who have loved us in life are only one dimension away. They come to us at critical moments to let us know that someone close to us is about to join them on the other side, and that even though their physical body has died their spirit lives on.

* * *

SEVEN

*"Our feet are planted in the real world, but
we dance with angels and ghosts."*
John Cameron Mitchell

Ghosts

When I was a child visiting my grandparents I heard my first story about a ghost. The story involved events surrounding the recent death of a relative who lived the "Old Country" of Poland, which was the ethnic origin of my family. The relative who died was a man, and in the days prior to his death the ghost of his deceased wife often visited him in the evening to adjust the blankets on his bed to give him comfort. The feeling among the family when they told this story, and the feeling I carried with me after I heard it, was, "This is scary!" For many years afterward I associated ghosts with fear.

But in both my personal and professional experience since then, I've changed the way I feel about such phenomena. While many dismiss ghostly experiences as dreams or delusion, I believe such events are another example of other dimensions opening into our reality under certain circumstances. There is commonality in the state of consciousness of someone perceiving a "ghost," and uniformity in the nature of what they see. The event mostly happens in the state between waking and sleeping when our torsion field is most activated and the spiritual visitor always appears in a similar fashion. Conversely, our own dissociation in this state can take us through a window in the veil to their reality, as well.

There are several reasons why ghostly entities travel back into our reality. One reason involves unfinished business; not completing closure of their life in this dimension, or simply to say goodbye. Perhaps it's to offer comfort to those left behind. Or it may also be that the continued presence of a spirit indicates that their death was so sudden, shocking, and unexpected that they find themselves frozen in a dream-like state and need assistance to move on. There are also many stories of ghosts or even voices coming forward to protect or save a loved one who is in danger on this side of existence.

 My friend, Sally, was having difficulty breathing one morning and she became quite aware that it was "hospital time." As her husband prepared to take her, she went to the bedroom to acquire important paperwork. As she was rummaging through papers, she heard this whispery voice say the word, *"Kidneys,"* quite clearly. She became so rattled by the experience that she dropped the search for paperwork and went immediately to the hospital. Once she was there, physicians were concentrating on a cardiac intervention. It wasn't until a couple days later that last of all it was discovered that she had kidney disease. It was obvious that some entity pierced the veil in order to give her that information up front. M E

Estelle was an employee at our non-profit agency who approached her work with energy and enthusiasm. She enlivened staff meetings with her jokes and laughter and it was a joy working with her. Like many of our trainees, however, the opportunity for a better position appeared and even though she left us, she kept in touch. When we learned later she'd developed cancer, we were deeply saddened. The disease was aggressive and moved quickly. When her doctor explained that there was nothing more he could do and that the end of her life was near, Estelle went home and fell into a coma shortly after.

On the day I heard this news, my last appointment involved relationship therapy with an especially difficult gay couple struggling with significant issues. Settled in my office, one partner who I will call John sat facing me while the other gentleman sat to the side. I was looking directly at John, ready to utter my first words, when I suddenly saw, from the corner of my eye, a black shape float into the room from the outer wall. I was rather shocked at what was happening but I kept looking straight at John and didn't turn for a better look. John turned his head abruptly and looked to his right, so I know that he saw it, too. But I believe he lost his view of the phenomenon when he turned. I continued watching the dark shape move slowly past me. It seemed to break into pieces that resembled an ink blot, but it kept moving toward my office door and then through it.

When I finished the therapy session, I sat in my office reflecting on my strange experience. Because the sad news about Estelle had been on my mind, I felt that what I had seen was Estelle herself come to say goodbye and take one more visit through the office. Because she had not yet died, what I experienced was an empathic near-death experience. Just as it was with my friend Jerry Chestnut, Estelle, as she prepared to die, was able to leave and then return to her dying physical body. I know that she had a special deep affection for me.

This experience was not over, however. Later that evening after dinner at home, my spouse Daniel and I sat in our hot tub to relax. I described to Dan what I believed had been my contact with Estelle that afternoon. Dan suddenly exclaimed, "Oh my God! There she is right above the pool!" We saw a dark, slightly-formed figure hovering over the swimming pool. I focused in that direction and said out loud how sorry we were that she was ill, and that we would miss her. I went on to say that we would understand if she had to leave. With that, the dark form shot upward and disappeared. Dan leaned back in the water with a look of shock on his face. Wide-eyed, he said, "You have to quit bringing ghosts home!"

A few days later I was working with a patient in my office in a quiet and comfortable therapy session. My state of consciousness was relaxed and peaceful. I glanced at the wall where I had seen Estelle's spirit before. To my surprise, standing slightly out from the wall was an unmoving faded gray geometric form. I knew at that moment Estelle had died and this was her final goodbye. Moments later a staff member came knocking on my door with the news. Before he said a word I said, "I know."

This event with my friend, Estelle, was not the last such experience I would have.

My patient, Louie, was having a tough time. He was divorced and had failed to form meaningful relationships with other women. He was in and out of therapy for years with one issue or another, and we had developed a mutual respect for each other. One of his problems concerned me deeply; he turned to alcohol when he was depressed, sometimes combined with tranquilizers. We created a treatment plan for Louie to help him manage his life and stresses with sobriety skills on the top of our list. I cautioned him that due to his compulsive personality, taking any first drink was a bad idea.

It was a Sunday evening around seven o'clock. As usual, Dan and I had finished dinner and were settling down to a movie. Dan pointed to the living room wall near the television and asked, "Where's that shadow coming from?" As I looked over, I saw a shapeless dark shadow moving across the wall. The shutters on the large front window were closed so there was no way a car's headlights from outside would have had any effect on the inside of our home. "I don't know," I said. Later, I thought that maybe someone had died.

Late in the afternoon, the next day at my office, I had a telephone call from Louie's son, Alex. He told me that when he arrived home on the previous evening he found his father passed out on the sofa and not breathing. He called paramedics and performed CPR until they arrived. Louie was pronounced dead at seven o'clock–within moments that Dan and I saw the inexplicable shadow move across our living room wall.

Sometimes when a person dies unexpectedly they leave things undone and may feel compelled to come back to visit. One such event in my own family was rather frightening at first, but viewed as benign as we analyzed the experience.

My maternal Great Grandmother, Barbara Sonnenburger, was born and raised in the elegant European capital of Vienna. In the late 19th century she and her father attempted to immigrate to the United States on an ocean liner after her mother had died. Enroute, it is believed that her father died of influenza. Barbara went back to Vienna, married Great Grandfather Andrew, emigrated successfully, and the family settled in Western Pennsylvania where Great Grandmother Barbara gave birth to several children.

Barbara was never happy with America where she lived next to a steel mill in Braddock, Pennsylvania. She was haunted by fond memories of her gracious childhood in Vienna and complained often to my Great Grandfather. Great Grandmother died in 1905 leaving her young children to grow up without their mother. Her unfinished business was her legacy of caring and being able to raise her children into adulthood. Family history describes Great Grandmother, Barbara, appearing from time to time including to my own mother, Barbara's granddaughter.

As my mother tells it, it was early morning and she was just waking up. Her consciousness was still in that place between waking and sleeping. Feeling very cold, she looked to the side of the bed and saw her Grandmother Barbara, dressed in a turn-of-the-century black and white attire, looking directly at her. Mom remembered such a black dress and white collar from family photographs and had no doubt this was Great Grandmother. Barbara was very animated as she looked at Mom and then said, referring to herself, "This is what you'll look like when you're old." Then she faded and vanished as Mom fully awakened.

For a long time after, Mom was quite frightened of that vision. But in retrospect, the experience likely was a loving communication from a grandmother whom Mom never knew.

Often a ghost makes itself known with the intention of helping loved ones in some way. My client, Walt, had such an experience that was profound.

Walt was a construction foreman who worked on tall steel structures for commercial buildings. One of the issues he brought to psychotherapy was family grief regarding the loss of his younger sister who had died suddenly of a brain aneurism when they were both in their early twenties.

Walt and his sister had been very close. He had never stopped missing her and this loss was the most serious event for both him and his family.

The particular day that will forever remain in Walt's memory was a Sunday. He was concerned about a structure on the construction site and made the decision to go and check an issue before work started on Monday morning. He arrived at the job site and spent a few moments in the mobile unit for the site out of a need to check some previous calculations and drawings. He took his time, enjoying the tranquility of the deserted site and arrived at his much-needed answers.

With drawings and calculations in hand Walt began walking towards the area of the building that reflected his concern. All of a sudden, looking out over the site and through the steel structure, Walt saw his sister standing in the distance. He blinked his eyes just to make sure that his vision was somehow real. She looked over, briefly made eye contact with Walt, and disappeared. Overcome with emotion, Walt ran back to the mobile unit and wept. He called his wife to relate the experience. Once composed, he got up and began walking towards the site. Just as he did so the earth began to rattle and a full blown California earthquake erupted. There were crashing sounds coming all around him.

As the rumbling stopped and the dust settled, Walt made the wise decision to curtail any further movement towards the building for the day. It became immediately aware to him that the portion of the building that had collapsed had been exactly where he was headed.

Walt knew instantly that his sister had appeared at that moment to save his life. If he had made it to the building in those first moments before the earthquake, he would have been crushed under the collapsed portion of the building.

I asked Walt what he learned from this incident. He told me, "I learned that even though people that we love may leave us, they're really not that far away and, most of all, they still care."

Another of my clients, "Wolf," had a similar experience that changed his attitude during a critical period in his life.

Wolf's full stage name was Wolfman. When he left his daytime employment, he enjoyed three or four nights a week as a raucous male dancer in a Las Vegas club. His ethnic background was Native American and he possessed a natural elegance that made him resemble a fashion model. On cold days he would walk into my office wearing a dignified black topcoat with a look that represented magazine material. His parents were both deceased and he always spoke of having wanted to be closer with his father, and that that part of his life felt unfinished. When his father died he took a marijuana cigarette to the mortuary and tucked it in the shirt pocket of the body prior to burial. "In the end," Wolf said, "Dad and I had a moment of true sharing!"

When Wolf was diagnosed with AIDS, he came to me for therapy. Despite the seriousness of his condition, Wolf had a quick wit and enjoyed joking during our conversations.

He came into session one day with a little more seriousness. "I've just had an unbelievable experience," he said. "My dad came to visit me last night. And I was totally un-medicated. In fact," he added, "it was two a.m. and it happened when I got up to *take* my medication." Wolf described coming out of his bedroom through the dining room to the kitchen where he kept his medication. "When I looked over at the dining room table," he said, "there was my dad sitting at the head of it. And this was not a wispy see-through kind of ghost! He appeared full-bodied and he smiled and told me he was thankful for the joint. Then he told me that he loved me and that I should take good care of myself and follow the doctor's orders. Then he faded and disappeared!"

"Or did you just wake up the rest of the way?" I thought.

This experience for Wolf was a harbinger of his functionality, because he did, indeed, strive afterward to take care of his health. He never lost his playful personality and during the last hours of his life he and his spouse invited me to become part of his "family of creation" who

70

loved and supported him when others had gone. As he lay in bed I remember that he had a deflated look. Peering up at me, he smiled and whispered, "Ronnie babe! Thank goodness you're here! You have to help me!" Looking at the friends around the bed he smiled and said. "I'm trying to die and these fuckers won't let me go!" He passed away the next morning and I'm sure he journeyed into the continuing peace that he felt with his father in those early hours of that special morning.

Unlike Walt's and Wolf's experiences, ghostly encounters sometimes can seem to have no reason at all beyond providing a momentary glimpse into the other dimension. My friend, Tommy, remembers such an experience when he was fifteen years old staying at his elderly aunt's comfortable old house while his parents were away.

One evening Tommy was relaxing on the living room sofa looking toward the foyer. Suddenly, as he watched, a woman dressed in white appeared from the area of the front door. She moved slowly across the foyer and disappeared down the hall. "It must be Aunt Alice playing a joke on me," he thought. He ran up to the second floor and found Aunt Alice sitting comfortably in her sewing room with alterations on her lap and needle in hand. "Aunt Alice, were you just downstairs with a strange outfit on?" he asked. "I'm here sewing and I've been here quite a while," she answered. With no apparent reason for such a visitation, the experience remains for Tommy one of the most unique events of his life.

One interesting modern aspect of ghostly encounters is how so many such images are easily captured by security cameras and digital photographs. That's because this medium is "broadband." Cameras can record more frequencies of energy than the human eye can see. Shortly after my father died, my brother, Ken, was taking digital pictures inside the house he and his wife shared with my parents. One photo captured an amazing image: my father sitting comfortably on a sofa in the back of the room "watching over" the family.

Further, digital media have captured variations in the shape and appearance of spirit entities, the most familiar of which are orbs. Some claim orbs are the result of light reflection on the camera lens. One such reflection may be possible, but less likely are the appearance of two, three, seven or more orbs in a digital photograph. A cousin recently snapped a digital photo as she was ascending the stairway in an old family home. Gathered at the top of the stairs were several brightly glistening orbs.

In discussing reasons for spirit encounter, the logistics of such events, or even the various appearances of these entities, I can only say that I wish I had more answers. What I do believe without dispute, however, is that what we call ghosts are a real phenomenon that many of us experience in moments when "need" opens a window in the veil, and those who are about to pass through or who have passed through before us, return momentarily to finish business or to let us know that they care.

* * *

EIGHT

"Dreams are the guiding words of the soul." Carl Jung

Dreams and Visions

Of the many ways through which we are given glimpses into other dimensions, the most common are dreams and visions.

A dream is the presentation of images accompanied by feelings while we're asleep. It's like a movie projected from the unconscious to the conscious mind and remembered afterward. Also, a dreamer may often participate in the action of their dream, like an actor in a film.

There are several kinds of dreams, as well. Sometimes, a dream is a disjointed experience composed of random images and feelings that may be associated with past memories, or we may not recognize them at all. They might be symbolic representations of elements in our lives or merely a fantasy concocted by our unconscious.

Another kind of dream presents images associated with a specific real-life event in which we have repressed our feelings. With this kind of dream, our unconscious mind is providing us with a debriefing opportunity and a path toward closure. Unfinished business can sometimes be resolved in therapy through deep examination of the information given in dreams like these.

Traumatic dreams and nightmares are often inspired by a traumatic event in our life that we have not resolved. These dreams can be precise in re-creating the event and our feelings at the time. Or the dream might present images that differ from the actual event, but the unresolved feelings are usually true and accurate. Such dreams, triggered by reminders of the traumatic event, can force us to relive that event over and over until therapeutic interaction intercedes to lead us to emotional closure and integration into the ordinary flow of our life's memories.

The most fascinating type of dream, however, is the precognitive dream that presents images, details, and feelings from a future event. These dreams are a glimpse into the next dimension where the past, present, and future exist simultaneously.

My neighbor, Riley, a Vietnam War veteran, needed me to accompany him to the Air Force Base Hospital in Las Vegas for hernia repair. I brought him home after surgery, had his prescription medication filled, gave him a light dinner, and made sure he was resting comfortably before I went home. Very early the next morning I had a dream about Riley. I was driving him somewhere in my car and had a feeling of urgency in the dream. We came to an intersection where I needed to turn left onto a four-lane thoroughfare. There was a young man standing in the intersection in full Air Force uniform directing traffic. Just then a red automobile shot across the highway from my left as I was about to turn and ran the airman down. After the car passed, the young man lay face down on the asphalt. I turned to Riley and said, "Oh my God, he's dead!" But then the airman stirred, stood up, and began directing traffic again. My last response in the dream was something like, "*Wow*, he's alive!"

Shortly after I awoke, Riley telephoned to say he was bleeding through his incision and needed to go back to the hospital. I picked him up and we headed down East Charleston Boulevard intending to turn left onto Nellis Boulevard towards the Air Force base. Just as we arrived at the intersection where I would turn, there was a grisly accident. Police were directing traffic while emergency vehicles were parked around the scene. A severely damaged red van sat in the far lane to our left. A motorcyclist had rammed into the right side at tremendous speed. The cycle and its driver were lodged in the van and emergency workers were attempting to extricate the young man. As they pulled the apparently lifeless body from the vehicle I turned to Riley and said, "Oh my God, he's dead."

Just as we began to move on, Riley noticed the motorcyclist's hand move and said, "Alive by the skin of his teeth." As we arrived at the Air Force base there was a young man in full Air Force uniform directing heavy Friday morning traffic. The movement of his arm mimicked the traffic director in the dream.

It wasn't until after I brought Riley home later that I had time to think about the dream I'd experienced and the fairly similar incident it foretold. While the dream images and the actual scene of the accident differed somewhat, all the essential elements were there: my driving Riley with a sense of urgency, the traffic accident, a red vehicle, someone directing traffic at the intersection, a young man apparently almost killed but stirring to life, and the words I said to Riley. It was clear that the emotional intensity of Riley's need to return to the hospital and the aftermath of the accident we would see on our way, forced a window from the next dimension to open and the information came to me through my dream.

Unlike dreams, which come to us during sleep and in which we often participate and respond emotionally, visions are an animated or non-animated picture of the past, present, or future that occur when a person is in an altered state of consciousness such as deep meditation or trance. Theta brain waves are the telling place. In such moments, consciousness and torsion fields can cross a barrier that leaves windows in the veil standing open and information from the next dimension comes through rather freely. When Marlene Kaminski [see chapter 5] performed a psychic reading for me she went into a trance while staring at my ring which lay on the table between us. In trance she saw images—visions–associated with my life that she described to me.

My own understanding of visions first developed in 1988 when I began my therapy practice. The first support group I formed was for families and significant others of persons who were living with AIDS. One of the group members, a gay man named Alan, asked if I would see his partner, Tommy, individually. Tommy was the first person with AIDS for whom I would facilitate psychotherapy. He was an insightful manager in the resort industry with a spring in his step, and it was hard to believe he was dealing with this difficult disease. But with a strong sense of connectedness between us, we rousted out and resolved some of his issues and then developed a strategy for telling his family that he was ill.

As his disease progressed, Tommy was hospitalized when he developed pneumocystis pneumonia. With twenty-four hour care and a dedicated physician, he soon regained his strength and some degree of wellness. But he was still haunted by his fear of how close he was to the end of his life. It's my theory that this fear caused Tommy to dissociate into an alternate state of consciousness and inspired a series of visions that that began while he was hospitalized and continued throughout the rest of his life. He always enjoyed painting a picture of his visions when he came to visit with me.

Tommy described his wake-sleep cycle as "all messed up" while he was in the hospital, and he would lie awake in the middle of the night drifting between what he described as alpha and theta brain wave activity. He described a sensation of feeling something "click" in his head and suddenly he was aware of his spiritual self rising out of his body. During these experiences the hospital appeared slightly foggy and unclear, yet Tommy could see through the walls down to the steel beams of the building. Feeling that he was on some kind of tether, he left the hospital and found himself in a place of warm darkness. What he described was "soul travel" where his spirit drifted into a different environment. These were not hallucinations, even though there are those who would swear by it. These were ordered, detailed visions with their own story that occurred in an altered state.

In his first such experience Tommy found himself floating over what he described as a French Renaissance mansion where there was a festive event in the ballroom. People were dressed in fashions of the 17th century: women wore full gowns and men wore white periwigs. Tommy heard music in the background and people were dancing in formation. A fireplace burned brightly. A man with a large bellows drew warm air from the fire to fill balloons for the children. The balloons drifted around the room where Tommy's consciousness was hovering. As he described his experience Tommy remembered it as "absolutely exquisite!"

He soon felt himself pulled back gently down through the hospital building into his body and bed. This was a vision in its truest form and was the first of many. To assuage his fear of dying the next dimension had just "guested" him to a lavish party that still lived in the archives of the past. Tommy came to love these visions and found them comforting. He explained that they taught him that there's more to existence than what appears to be right here, right now. It was good for him to know that, and good for me too.

As time passed, Tommy grew more and more ill. There was a point when he could no longer come to the office for appointments, so we developed a standing appointment at his home each Wednesday at 1:00 p. m. Since I had to travel from the east to the west side of town, I often combined my visit to Tommy with a stop in the AIDS unit of University Medical Center to see my clients who were ill. One day stands out in my memory. It was about 12:50 p. m. as I left the AIDS unit and walked to my car. I had just enough time to drive to Tommy's for our appointment. Just then my pager began beeping. When I pushed the display button there was no number recorded for me to call back, so I drove on to my appointment.

Tommy's spouse, Alan, met me at the door looking wrung out and exhausted. "Tommy just died," he said. As I walked into the living room I saw Tommy's mother, Ilene, sitting by her son's body. She made a place for me beside her, and for a few moments Alan, Ilene, and I sat in silence and had our own quiet wake. Later, as Alan walked me to the door, I asked him, "Did you page me?" "No," he answered. Afterward I realized my pager signaled in at the exact moment that Tommy died. I couldn't help but wonder if Tommy, having been so experienced at being out of his body during his hospital visions, hadn't come to give my pager a tickle.

Before she returned home to California, Tommy's mother stopped by my office to visit. She knew about her son's visions and told me he was disappointed when they didn't happen more often. Two days after Tommy died; she experienced a vision of her own. As she sat quietly in the living room, in a state between waking and sleep, an open doorway appeared in front of her surrounded by silver light. There was also light beyond the doorway as well. While she couldn't see Tommy, Ilene knew he was on the other side. "I could hear his voice," she said. "He was doing exactly what he loved most. He was telling a story in a once-upon-a-time fashion and sharing something important!"

As evidence of communication between our life and the next dimension, dreams and visions are among the most common and powerful, both providing vehicles for healing and affirmation. As for Tommy, I hope that as he journeyed out of his body on that last occasion, he "hooked up" with one of the parties he experienced in his visions and that he is no longer just a perceiver, but a full participant as he travels through the timelessness of the next dimension.

* * *

NINE

"Living with multiple personalities is not something you just wake up fully understanding. For months, maybe years after I first accepted the diagnosis, I was discovering new nuances, fresh areas I hadn't considered." Kim Noble

Multiple Identities - Multiple Souls: Dissociative Identity Disorder

In June 2000 the American Psychiatric Association changed its former diagnosis of Multiple Personality Disorder to Dissociative Identity Disorder (DID). This makes better sense as it is not different personalities a person with DID experiences, but whole and separate identities that such individuals possess. One patient with DID to whom I offered treatment told me that one of their identities had allergies while others did not. It's been shown that each identity in a dissociative identity experience has a different brain wave pattern. Blood flow patterns, muscle tone, heart rate, posture and facial features may also vary. I've witnessed alter identities with different eye color: one might have blue eyes while another has green. I've marveled at how alter identities have different hand writing and verbal accents. At one point one of my female clients switched from her everyday plain English-speaking host identity to a woman with a thick southern accent. When I questioned that alter identity, she explained that she had lived in the New Orleans when she came into being. One of my male clients, frequently changes from pure English speaking into an alter identity with a flowing Italian brogue. Through my own experience, it has also been clear to me that persons having this experience possess psycho-kinetic abilities and can move objects. Yes, that's what I said; they can move objects!

At first, when a DID experience manifests in an individual, the host identity (usually the identity with whom the person is born) does not know that the others are there and the host is simply aware of lost time when one of the other identities is occupying the body. In these moments when an alter identity is "out" and occupying the body, the host, in turn, will have no memory of what that identity does or says. Since a barrier of amnesia exists between the identities, such events are remembered only by the one who was present and inhabiting the body at that time. I believe that some alter identities, except for a minimal connection, may exist entirely outside of the host's body as an energy form with a spiritual nature of their own and perhaps their own torsion field and consciousness. The DID experience has psychological, spiritual and physical manifestations. Most textbooks I've read about this phenomenon avoid noting anything that could indicate a trans-dimensional element. However, I believe it's almost impossible for an individual to dissociate as much as DID's do without having a window into the next dimension. One of the therapists at our agency was shocked when she expressed one of her beliefs to her DID patient. The patient looked at her and said, "Your grandfather agrees with you!" The therapist's grandfather had been dead for twenty years, and had indeed shared his granddaughter's opinion. The DID patient had no way of knowing this without access to the other dimension.

The common element of DID is severe trauma. When an individual is traumatized they suffer an emotional breaking point. They feel threatened with death or complete decompensation, and find relief in a dissociative trance. It is within this trance state that a new identity is born who can endure and survive whatever trauma is happening at the time. When the newly formed identity reaches its own level of intolerable threat, the dissociation and identity formation process happens again. Each of these identities remains present in the host's brain, mind, and consciousness, and will reappear again when an environmental or emotional trigger occurs. A DID person can dissociate continually in the midst of trauma. While most persons with DID have anywhere from eight to thirteen different identities,[16] I've worked with an individual who was diagnosed with nearly a hundred. Further, I question the word "disorder." Is it a disorder or is it simply a dissociative identity "experience" that speaks to a built-in defense mechanism that keeps one from complete mental and emotional disintegration? Is this dissociative adjustment to a terrorizing event a pathology or a helpful phenomenological experience?

In treating DID, there are two goals toward resolution: incorporation or integration.

Incorporation is achieved when all barriers of amnesia between the alter identities have been removed through psychotherapy, and an intimate "mode of corroboration" develops among all of them. "Mode of corroboration" refers to the group of identities making mutual decisions regarding the times when one identity versus another can be present and in control of the body. For instance, a "child" identity that comes out when the adult alter identity is on the job can be disastrous. Incorporation therapy is meant to avoid such situations.

Integration is achieved when all the alternate identities have received intensive psychotherapy to deal with past trauma, and they are ready and willing to be joined into one. This process can be facilitated under hypnosis by invoking an altered state of consciousness. Alter identities are born in an altered state of consciousness and will essentially be "unborn" in such a state. Once integrated, a new identity is formed that incorporates parts of the alter identities. The mother of one of my patients often tells me, "I don't know who I'm talking to anymore!" Her daughter has received extensive therapy. All barriers of amnesia between her alter identities have been obliterated and they seem to be "melting together" over time.

Of the many DID clients I've treated in my career, the one whose case most stands out in my memory is a young woman named Marie.

Marie had been referred by her physician who had deep concerns for her well-being. She had both an alcohol problem and nearly suicidal depression. Having experienced some health problems meant that her level of drinking was destructive to her body, since alcohol is one of the most dangerous drugs. At the beginning of her treatment plan, Marie and I made a mutual agreement that she must become totally sober. She was a willing patient and within thirty days had established sobriety. Her mood lifted and she looked and felt better. On occasion, she would appear in group therapy where she dealt with continuing recovery issues.

But Marie's deeper story began during a brief afternoon conversation we shared during one of her therapy sessions. "I'm feeling slightly better," she said, "But there's something wrong with me that has me really confused, and it's been that way for a long time. The drinking helped bury it." She explained that she'd been having "memory problems." "This morning my mother told me that we spent most of yesterday at the mall, but I don't remember a thing."

Except for some lingering depression, Marie's life had seemed to normalize. But she was clearly undergoing some kind of dissociative experience. Sometimes in session she seemed to go "somewhere else." I could see her eyes change. Suspecting DID, I tailored my questions.

"Have you lost the memory of days in the past?" I asked.

"All the time."

"Do you ever lose smaller blocks of time, such as a few hours here and there? In other words it might be twelve noon, and all of a sudden it's five p.m. and you have no idea what happened in between?"

"Yes," she said. "And sometimes I have this waking-up experience in front of someone else and I have no idea why I'm there or what we were talking about. I try to play along with the situation but I often feel like a fool and very confused when this happens. I've tried to explain this to my family but they just look at me like I'm crazy. You seem to be the only one that understands or has some idea what I might be going through. I just want to know what's wrong with me."

It was obvious that Marie was describing Dissociative Identity Disorder, but I continued with questions just to be certain.

"Do others ever describe things that you've done or said for which you have no memory?" I asked.

"My mother and I get into arguments all the time. When I tell her that I don't remember, she thinks I'm lying."

I asked a last question that I probably didn't phrase in the best way. "Do you ever feel like there's someone else there with you and that you are not alone in this body or in your life?"

"Oh, yes! Sometimes I hear a voice that sounds way far away. I can't quite make out what it's saying. I feel *haunted*."

Once I was certain Marie was having a dissociative identity experience I explained the phenomenon to her as thoroughly as I could. Afterward, we talked in more detail about her background.

Like all stories of abuse, hers were difficult to hear. Her mother had been married several times and at least two of her husbands had brutally abused Marie physically and sexually. I learned that from a very early age she had developed alter identities as her abuse continued. Now that I was fully aware, it was my job, along with Marie, to plot a course for DID therapy.

Our first step was to bring her alter identities to the surface and understand the circumstances under which they manifested. The next step would be to determine the time frames in which manifestation occurred. Each identity would need its own treatment plan and psychotherapy.

Initially, I discovered 10 identities different in gender, chronological age, and sexual orientation. Millie was an impetuous little girl about seven years old. She would hide objects that belonged to others and watch while family members struggled to find them. Dow, short for Dowager was a seventy-five-year-old woman who liked to dress up in a very old fashioned way and wear classic jewelry like broaches. Gigi was a sensual woman who wore long, flowing dresses. An identity named May told me that she was the "manager" of Marie's alter identity system, a category that clinically we refer to as an "internal self-helper."

Because there was constant conflict between Marie and her mother, I requested a family session. When I explained the DID experience to Marie's mother, she looked relieved and understood that Marie was not lying when she said she didn't remember certain events and conversations because an alter identity occupied her body at the time. Once her mother understood what was happening to her daughter, their home life improved dramatically. Her mother understood and had conversations with the alter identities.

Marie continued to astonish me and I remember one defining moment in our course of treatment when I learned something that suggested a trans-dimensional aspect to the dissociative identity experience.

On this particular morning I was working with May, the internal self-helper, when all of a sudden she went into trance, indicating a change in the alter identity. She raised her head and her eyelids fluttered. The energy surrounding her reflected a softness. Where May could be intense and sharp-edged in her relation to me, the emerging identity was measured and calm. I knew that this was someone I had not spoken with before.

"Good morning," I said. "Do you know who I am?"

"I know you, Ron," the new identity said. The changes in body language were smooth and dignified.

"Who are you?" I asked.

"I represent the Light and I come from the place that you call God. My name is Judith."

I was speechless. One of my mentors who treated persons with DID told me once that there could be psychotic identities who really believed they represented some deity.

"Tell me more about you," I said.

"My purpose here is to watch over Marie and help her when she needs me."

"Are you a guardian angel?"

"Actually," Judith said, "If you prefer to use that terminology for me, that's acceptable. You may not be aware of this, but Marie's grandparents, her mother's parents are deceased. I was sent by them to watch over her."

"When did you first come to be? Or should I ask, what were the circumstances under which you were sent?"

"It was a terrible time for Marie," Judith told me. "Everyone in the system was crashing because they couldn't handle what was going on. Marie was in a terrible situation with her drunken stepfather and he was doing considerable harm to her. I took over the body, reached for a phone and dialed a quick 911 while kicking away at the stepfather. The police merely showed up and Marie was safe. Stepfather went to jail."

"You talk about coming down and entering the body," I said. "Where is it that you usually hang out?"

"I'm always just a slight distance above Marie's body so I can enter quickly if I need to. The only time I'm away from her is if I go to confer with those on the other side who care about her."

"So you stay outside of Marie's body?"

"Yes."

"And what do you mean by other side?"

"In your concepts, it's the next place beyond this one. Some people might see it as part of Heaven. It's the first place your spirit goes when you die. Time does not exist in this place. Sometimes when people die they remain there and wait until the one that they love on this side also passes. Once the loved one passes, they can move on together, to a reality that's beyond the one I've just described."

"Does Marie know you exist?" I asked.

"No, but May does."

When Marie's session was over, I sent her and her alter identity system home with the internal self helper, May, safely driving the car. As I debriefed afterward, I still thought Judith might be a psychotic personality.

Over the next month Marie and I followed a standard course of treatment for DID. She and her identities came and went a couple times per week—but I soon would change my mind about Judith.

My friend, Jerry Chestnut, died on April 18, 1994. I was emotionally distraught as I managed taking care of Jerry's affairs and was a bit dissociated myself. A couple of days later Marie came to my office for a therapy session. After facilitating treatment with Marie's child alter identities, I checked in with Judith. As she manifested she looked at me with great concern. "I'm so sorry Ron," she said. "Someone very close to you has just died and it's been very sad for you."

"How is it that you know this?" I asked Judith.

"He's standing beside you and what I sense from him is that he isn't ready to leave yet. He's going to hang around for a while. He wants to make sure that you're okay."

Jerry himself frequently told me that when he died he was going to spiritually stick around a while to be sure I would be all right. What I heard from Judith, then, suggested to me there were windows between this dimension and the next and that this alter identity, as Judith, was passing through one of those windows. This became undeniable to me as Marie's course of treatment continued. At one point I was concluding a session when Judith looked at me and said, "I know you treat other people with multiple personalities."

"That's true," I said. "But how is that known to you?"

"Most multiples can recognize other multiples. Their auras appear with a layer for each personality. We can tell that there's more than one person there. There's a man you treat who has a personality by the name of Wick," Judith said. "It sounds like a plain name, but Wick really stands for Wicked, and I know that this is a fierce, personality that protects that person."

This was absolutely true and Judith had no way of knowing that.

"How does this information come to you?" I asked.

"Just like I'm the one who watches over Marie, the one who watches over the other person leaves a little bit of himself behind after he visits. And I get my information from that." I wondered if this phenomenon wasn't precise evidence for the existence of the torsion field. It's a though the other person's torsion field with representation of his guardian, left a smudge of himself in my office after he left, and Judith could read from that.

"I also see that you treat another woman as well," Judith said.

"What can you tell me about her?"

"She has an alternate personality by the name of Sally, and the suffering that this person has experienced is unimaginable. She has a great many different personalities and from what I can tell it's probably in the upper eighties."

I did indeed have a young woman who had been released to me from one of the local psychiatric facilities where she had been diagnosed with eighty-seven separate identities.

I called Marie back into her body and concluded our session.

As it happened, I had scheduled the other young woman with the Sally identity–host name Margaret–right after Marie. When I walked Marie into the reception area I saw Margaret waiting. Marie stopped in her tracks and stared directly at Margaret. "Hello," she said to Margaret with a note of alarm. "You're in trouble. You haven't slept for a couple days. What's going on?" I wondered if Judith had come forward with the specific purpose of speaking with Margaret. I decided the two needed to be alone and said, "You two talk for a bit and I'll come for Margaret in a few minutes." I am a stickler for protecting the confidentiality of my patients, but I certainly had no control over the recognition process claimed by these individuals.

In future sessions with Marie and Margaret, I affirmed that prior to that moment they had never met or seen each other. I do know that whatever was being worked through in the moment they met, Marie (or Judith) was a great help to Margaret. And Marie confessed that it was the presence of layered visible auras that made Margaret stand out.

As time passed, Marie improved. I followed the incorporation resolution plan for her. We slowly obliterated the barriers of amnesia that existed between the alternate identities in her system so each knew the others existed. I contrived the metaphor of an internal conference room where all the identities could gather to make agreements about which of them could be present and inhabiting Marie's body at a given time. I considered this to be a preliminary step to integration. Her anxiety levels and that of all the alter identities decreased considerably. Along the way I continued my check-ins with Judith. By now I knew and accepted that she was a spiritual being with one foot in this reality and the other in the next dimension. She talked about the timelessness of the next dimension and that when one entered that place there were answers to all questions, which suggested the Akashic Record as a spiritual concept where the answers to all questions exist. I'd heard that often from my clients who were major dissociatives.

One afternoon I asked Judith, "What happens when people die?"

"Well," she said, "to me, reincarnation is a fact. We come into this existence to learn and perfect ourselves spiritually. When we pass over, we go to a place, which, in your understanding, would be like a class room. We examine our life, its learning and meaning, with entities that I will refer to as the Wise Ones. Then a mutual decision is made regarding whether the spirit goes back for more learning or moves on to a higher place." Judith explained that sometimes there's a pause in the process so we can wait for someone we love to cross over. "Death can be so scary to the experiencer," she added. "When it's time for someone to cross over, three entities are sent. As they stand at the bed, the spirit in the middle takes the spiritual hand of the person who's crossing, and the two on either side offer reassurance. During times when I'm not watching over Marie, I am one of the beings that will stand on either side and offer reassurance. There is only one bridge between this side and the other and that is love.

Judith also helped me understand the final passing of my friend, Jerry Chestnut. Each morning before I headed into my office I took time to meditate in our rose garden at home. One morning in July 1994, three months after Jerry had died, I was meditating. About halfway through my meditation I sensed something near me go "whoosh" and move away. I wondered what had just happened and realized it had been Jerry taking his final leave of me. There was no doubt in my mind that this was so. I sat in silence for a while and wished him peace and bon voyage. Then I went on to the office.

I had a telephone call from Marie later that day. She said, "This is important. Judith says that she needs to speak to you!" So I scheduled an afternoon meeting. As soon as she walked in, I knew from her body language that this was not Marie. She said, "It's me Judith. I'm the one here today." May was often the first alter identity with whom Marie came in, but never Judith.

"I'm glad that you could come," I said. "This must be really important."

"It's about you, Ron. And it's about your friend; the one who passed, the one that was standing beside you. He wants you to know that he's aware that you're doing okay and that he's left."

"And when was that, Judith?"

"This morning," she said.

"Where is it that he's gone?

"He's crossed a barrier and moved on to a higher place. He's gone to another level. He won't be coming back here."

"What might that place be like?"

Judith hesitated then told me, "I can't say because those of us that dwell in the next place from here are not given that information. That information is given to no one. All I can tell you is that he journeyed on and he was happy." Judith came over and hugged me. I wished her well and sent her on her way.

Judith's message was important for me to hear not only because she affirmed what I had felt earlier that day about Jerry, but affirmed as well, my growing belief in the reality of Spirit, whatever it entails, despite the scientifically proven evidence-based methods of my work in psychotherapy. What an experience! I offered healing to Marie and Judith took care of me. This certainly wasn't "by the book!"

After delivering her message about Jerry, I never saw Judith—or Marie—again. Marie never kept her next appointment, nor did I see her out in the community after that, like I sometimes had in the past. I did not make phone calls or run after her. The incorporation had been a success. She was gone; never to be seen again.

And the Angel had taken her leave.

* * *

TEN

*"You can't choose between life and death when
we're dealing with something in between."*
Tangina Barrons

Dissociative Identity Disorder:
The Phenomenon of Remote Influence

There is another aspect to Dissociative Identity Disorder that might serve as the "twist" in stories of paranormal phenomenon such as reports of ghost sightings, psychokinetic activity, and poltergeists. I suspected this while I was treating a troubled couple who had been together for many years.

It was fear that brought Rob and Arnie into therapy. The couple had moved to Las Vegas from Ohio. Arnie had an alcohol problem that Rob had long been aware of and endured. But when Rob came home from work late one evening, something happened that not only indicated that Arnie's drinking was getting worse, but it terrified Rob. He found Arnie in the kitchen, deeply drunk. Arnie merely stared at Rob, silent, while the expression on his face was full of rage and hate. His face and eyes were red and Rob was afraid Arnie would lash out at him physically. Rob maintained his composure and said, "You need to go to bed, Arnie." At this point Rob knew better than to try to reason with him when he was under the influence. Rob spent the night in their spare bedroom sleeping restlessly.

The next morning Arnie behaved as though nothing had happened and he didn't know why Rob spent the night in the spare bedroom. Over breakfast, Rob explained what had happened and then announced,

"Either we go into therapy and deal with your alcoholism or I'm out of this house and out of this relationship!"

When Rob and Arnie arrived at our agency, an assessment revealed that Arnie had crossed the boundary of increasing alcohol tolerance into addiction. Sober for two days prior, Arnie trembled from withdrawal. Rob presented as a classic co-dependent whose tolerance for Arnie's addiction had increased over the years as Arnie's addiction grew worse–until that moment in their kitchen two days before when Rob faced Arnie's demonic expression.

Arnie's and Rob's case was a textbook version of addiction and co-dependence. Both men adamantly denied any psychiatric problems or traumatic experiences from the past. Neither one had had any previous long-term relationships. I referred Arnie to an addictions therapist and arranged separate appointments with me for Rob who was in a mild depression. Once each had acquired a grip on the theme of his own recovery, we would bring the couple together for relationship therapy and hopefully set a strong path for their future.

While Arnie's progress was difficult with periods of sobriety and relapse, working with Rob was a pleasure. After several weeks of processing, a strong therapeutic bond developed between us. Rob was an avid patient and devoured the reading material I gave him. He did very well with his own recovery in recognizing and dealing with his codependency issues and his role as enabler of Arnie's drinking. Sometimes our conversations spanned a wide variety of subjects. One day Rob explained that there were some "freaky" things that had happened in his and Arnie's home that he wanted to talk about.

"Do you believe in haunted houses?" Rob asked.

"I don't have a solid opinion and I definitely have no experience," I said.

Rob explained that it was not just their houses he often felt were haunted but that he was himself haunted, as well. "It began back in Ohio," he told me.

He and Arnie had purchased their first home together, an old Dutch Colonial dwelling that was a true fixer upper. One day while Arnie was at work, Rob was in the basement stripping the finish from a desk when he clearly heard someone walk up the basement stairs. "When I turned to look, there was no one there. Yet, I clearly heard the thud of a foot on each step." There was also loud knocking which frequently came from a first-floor room. Rob, more shocked than afraid when these phenomena happened, also described feeling "frustrated and alone" because Arnie dismissed the stories when Rob described them.

When Rob and Arnie moved to Las Vegas, Arnie's alcoholism worsened. At the same time, the paranormal phenomena that Rob had experienced in Ohio reappeared and increased not only in their new home but in Rob's own vicinity away from home. While filling out an employment application in the lobby of a small company where he wanted a job, the chair next to Rob suddenly moved six feet along the floor with a loud dragging noise. The receptionist watched the event and made a shocked remark that she'd never seen anything like that in her life. "I was also stunned," Rob said, and wondered about the source of these strange events. When he described these events to Arnie, he didn't believe Rob. "He was no help," Rob said.

There were other events and other witnesses. When Rob's parents visited, they heard intense knocking on the living room walls. Rob's and Arnie's house sitter, Joe, distinctly heard someone walking on the roof of the house, much like Rob's experience with the basement stairs. When he went outside to investigate, there was no one there. Once, working at his desk in the living room, a woman laughed into Rob's ear. "It was a deep, full-bodied laugh," Rob said. Yet another time, alone in a physician's waiting room, Rob watched a potted plant lift a foot off the floor and come back down with a loud bang and spin like a top until it came to rest. The only person left out of these experiences, Rob explained, was Arnie, who was always at work or away when the events occurred.

At one point when Arnie's therapist noted that Arnie had been in a sustained period of sobriety, and I felt that Rob had a good handle on his own issues, we put aside our discussions of paranormal activity and brought the couple together for therapy. I hoped we could help them shape themselves into a sober-living, individuated and healthier couple. Working toward healing their relationship, we established what their strengths were as a couple. They shared an Eastern European origin; their respective families accepted and supported their relationship; their home was a place of pride and order for them—except when Arnie's drinking went out of control. They enjoyed traveling to New York for Broadway musicals. There were many strengths and I felt we were off to a great start in couple's therapy, moving toward their mutual recovery.

But just before their fourth session, Rob called to cancel. Arnie had relapsed. We went back to individual counseling to process the circumstances around Arnie's relapse before moving ahead.

One evening when I was working late at the agency, the receptionist buzzed to tell me that Rob was in the reception area looking very distraught. His face was flushed, his eyes red and swollen. He'd obviously been crying and said, "Arnie died this morning. He never woke up. The paramedics said he had a massive heart attack." Rob calmed down and described how shocked and devastated he was. "We were repairing our lives. How could this happen?" As we wrapped up our session, I knew that Rob's healing and grief process would take months and perhaps always be an issue in his life in some way. Arnie had gone on to the next dimension and Rob's future had been drastically changed. Vera, a childhood friend of Arnie's, took time away from her work back East to stay with Rob as he dealt with family and Arnie's funeral. A week afterward, both came to the agency.

Rob was doing as well as anyone could under such circumstances, and there was an inkling that he was thinking a bit about how he would move on. He intended to continue taking care of the home he and Arnie had shared, and to devote himself to his job in the resort industry, which he loved. Vera promised to stay in close contact even though she lived across the country.

At some point in this session Rob described a paranormal event he'd just experienced. He'd been rummaging through a box of Arnie's belongings in a closet searching for a favorite videotape. This closet had a door which, when opened, would catch on the thick carpet and required some force to close. While digging through the box, Rob's fingers brushed what he thought might be Arnie's video—and at that moment, the closet door closed firmly, trapping Rob inside, trembling with a sudden deep chill. He left in a hurry and stayed away from the closet for the rest of the day. When he went back the next day to retrieve the videotape, he found it was indeed the one he'd been searching for and had touched. "Then I had this bizarre thought," he said. "Could that closing door be Arnie's spirit telling me I had the right tape?"

Listening to this story, I remembered that one of my teachers told me that persons with multiple identities often had psychokinetic abilities. Could such abilities briefly live on after that person has gone? I also knew that persons with Dissociative Identity Disorder can constantly relapse on drugs and alcohol because they have identities who are addicts. To assist such an individual into true sobriety, each identity has to be treated. On a hunch I asked Rob and Vera, "Did either of you ever see any abrupt changes in Arnie's personality and the way he portrayed himself?"

Both said, "All the time." And both described instances when Arnie exhibited a little boy identity with body language, voice, and mannerisms to match. Both had thought Arnie was only playing with them, and Rob had attributed the behavior to Arnie being drunk.

Now I felt I was definitely on to something; a key to Arnie's problems and perhaps an explanation of the paranormal experiences that had surrounded Rob, but which had never involved Arnie. I asked, "Do either of you know whether Arnie could have had traumatic experiences when he was young?"

While Rob had no idea, Vera began crying.

"There was a secret," she said, "that Arnie asked me never to reveal. Years ago, one night when he'd been drinking, he told me about something awful in his childhood. Because Arnie's mother had been sickly after she gave birth to him, and because he was the youngest of seven children, she turned him over to a babysitter and her husband who were childless. Arnie stayed with the sitter for long periods of time throughout his childhood. Both of them sexually abused him," Vera explained. "The wife went along with her pedophile husband and was a willing accomplice and participated in the rapes. They always gave him alcohol to settle him down before they abused him."

My suspicion was confirmed. The identity Rob and Vera had often seen was a drunken child. This explained not only that Arnie likely suffered from Dissociative Identity Disorder, but the reason why he had such difficulty attaining sobriety—he wasn't the only one living in his body that had an alcohol addiction. Vera's revelation also explained something else that Rob had experienced with Arnie but did not understand. Years before, the babysitter, an old woman by then who was widowed and confined to a wheelchair, had wanted to see Arnie. Arnie, with a bouquet of flowers, took Rob with him for the visit.

"When we arrived at her apartment," Rob remembered, "they had a conversation I didn't understand. She looked up at him, cried, and said that she was sorry about the past. Arnie accepted her apology, handed her the flowers, and kissed her forehead. Then he told her that it was a long time ago and not to worry about the past. When we were in the car on the way home, I asked him about the conversation. He only said, 'Never you mind!' There's no way I could have helped him because I didn't know the truth."

I explained Dissociative Identity Disorder to Rob and Vera, including its causes and manifestations.

"This is all so clear," Rob said. "But does the affected person hear voices?"

"They do," I explained "Often times the barriers of amnesia between identities start to leak. The voices of the other identities will be heard internally."

"The reason I ask," Rob continued, "is that as Arnie experienced periods of sobriety he complained of hearing a woman's voice. I asked him what the voice was saying and he said he couldn't understand the words. I just shrugged it off by telling him that the house was haunted. I reminded him of the female voice that laughed in my ear."

I explained that this is what happens when the barriers of amnesia between identities begin dissolving. But Rob's reminding of the laughter in his ear led me to think about the other paranormal phenomena he and others had experienced that Arnie had never experienced nor believed: the disembodied footsteps, the moving chair, the knocking, the closet door closing by itself. This was when I began developing the idea that many of these phenomena were about "remote influence."

Each identity attached to a person experiencing DID may have its own spiritual nature and consciousness that, like the host's nature, can express itself through the torsion field. This expression can project itself outside the host body, through the torsion field, and manifest elsewhere as what we call ghostly manifestations or poltergeist activity. Further, the more deeply the identities are submerged in the host's psyche, the more powerfully they scream to emerge, and that scream manifests as paranormal activity associated with the host body, not necessarily directly involving the host, but often involving those who are intimately connected to the host. "And that may have been the knocking on the walls and the movement of the chair in the employment lobby," I told Rob.

Rob nodded understandingly and said, "That red-faced red-eyed being who inspired me to insist we come into therapy wasn't really Arnie."

"No it wasn't," I agreed. "Identities that are part of a multiple's system usually each play a specific role. It sounds like this identity, although appearing demonic, was a protector personality for Arnie. Such personalities often appear vicious and frightening because they come into existence to fight off abusers."

Rob then described another incident when he left on an errand before Arnie awoke, and when he came back he found Arnie sitting at the kitchen table with a baffled look on his face. "When he got up," Rob said, "he couldn't figure out where I was and he didn't know where *he* was. He asked me if this was our house. Now I understand Arnie woke up in a different identity. He was very affectionate and strange all that day. That night he did some drinking and the next day he was back to Arnie. Now it all makes sense." Before he and Vera left my office that day we lit a candle and had a few moments of silence for Arnie. It was a wish for peace for him and all of the identities that were associated with him.

While Rob regretted not being able to help Arnie because he never knew his partner's childhood trauma, I regretted not having recognized Arnie's DID in time to treat him. However, I worked with Rob further to help him adjust to his life without Arnie and to better understand what happened during their life together.

Three years after Rob and I concluded therapy, I was at the supermarket when I heard someone call my name. It was Rob, who approached and gave me a big hug. He explained that he was well and deeply involved in the business of life. More important, he wanted me to know that all the strange phenomena had stopped: no more knocking or moving chairs and plants.

"Things are peaceful with me," he said "And I feel that Arnie's at peace too, wherever he is!"

* * *

ELEVEN

"This life is but a brief tenure, one of many perspectives a spirit must experience in the quest for eternity." Brian Rathbone

Repeat Performances: Reincarnation or Disembodied Memory?

Priscilla was a joy to have in therapy because her issues concerned personal growth and being with her was fun. The pastel colors she wore expressed her basic happiness and our sessions were always fulfilling. Our work had been successful and after a year of therapy our time together was coming to an end. It was at one of our last sessions that Priscilla brought up an issue that had long intrigued me but which had never yet, up to this point, shown itself in my practice.

"I want to share something with you," she said, "and I hope you don't think I'm crazy!"

"I'll do my best!" I told her. "Go right ahead."

"Well …… I chose my mother!"

"How is it you were able to do that?"

"I have memories of the time before I was born," Priscilla said. "I was just out there floating around and I was in this movie theater and began watching a young woman. I realized she was pregnant. She had such a warm and loving expression on her face that I decided I would go in and be that baby. And when I look at my mom today, she is exactly the person I thought she would be when I was just a spirit. I was right to choose her for my mom because she's never let me down."

This was the first time I heard such a story and I was eager to talk about it. "It appears to me," I said, "that you were in between spirit life and physical life. It's great to have that kind of a memory!"

"Then you don't think I'm crazy?"

"Who am I to doubt you? I think there's much we don't understand about the human experience, including trans-dimensional phenomena like you've just described." I thought of Priscilla's story in terms of reincarnation, so I asked her about it. "Do you have memories of anything before that moment in the movie theater?"

"I don't," she said. "All I remember is floating out there through the movie theater and seeing the woman I chose to be my mom."

I recently had another experience that reminded me of Priscilla's story. I was sitting in the sanctuary of the retreat center in Joshua Tree, California listening to a fascinating lecture by Jason Quitt, author of *Forbidden Knowledge: Revelations of a Multi-dimensional Time Traveler*[15]. Like Priscilla, Quitt discussed a pre-birth memory that was "as though" he was in a movie theater, saw the man and woman who would be his parents, witnessed their lives, and then "chose" them as his own. Priscilla's and Quitt's stories, similar, yet decades apart, suggested universality to such experiences. Quitt said he believed we've all had such an experience but most of us don't remember.

In thinking over the concept of reincarnation as suggested by Priscilla's and Quitt's memories, and other stories I've heard in therapy, I have many questions and observations. It has been explained that the purpose of living multiple lives is eventually to achieve spiritual perfection through physical life lessons. Does a spiritual entity reincarnate continuously until all lessons are learned, after which the entity travels on to a higher dimension? What is that higher dimension? Or, as what happened to Priscilla and Jason, does a spiritual entity who may have lived a previous physical life merely float around until they find a physical being with whom to connect, after which they relinquish their memories of that life as lived previously to that being?

Even more intriguing—do we, particularly as children living in a theta state of consciousness–tap into someone else's memories that may be filtering through the veil between this dimension and the next, and believe them to be our own? There are testimonies from children all over the world alluding to languages, knowledge, experiences, and skills that are impossible for them to know or possess at such young ages. Or, associated with this idea, could someone who has suffered trauma become a dissociative who is particularly receptive to the life memories of other entities that exist in the other dimension?

My patient, Mario, came into therapy after a near-miss construction accident. We dealt with his trauma successfully over a period of several weeks. But before we ended our sessions, Mario said, "I want to run something by you and get your opinion. Do you believe in reincarnation?" I told him I was learning and willing to hear about any such experiences my patients may have had.

Mario and his wife, Mary, toured Ireland shortly after their marriage. When they arrived in a small village in the countryside, Mario was gripped by a series of powerful emotional feelings. "I felt a deep sense of confusion," he said. "I felt that I'd been there before–but I had never been to Ireland." Mario and his wife took a room in a hotel nearby and then sat together in the village square. "This was a place where I had lived," Mario told me, "But not in this life. I walked along the narrow street. In the deepest place in my heart, I knew that I had walked this street as a boy; an Irish boy named Freddie. I cried as memory flooded my thoughts. There were childhood games and errands for parents that all took place here, on this narrow street." Mario could not sleep that night as his mind filled with images of his past in this village. He also experienced visions of terrible World War II combat which he believed is what ended Freddie's life. The next morning he and Mary drove to what he knew to have been his boyhood home where he was certain his mother and sister from that life may have still lived. He cried with anguish over whether to approach them but decided it would be too overwhelming for all of them. "I let it go because I felt they had already grieved." Mario himself, all these years later, as he sat in therapy with me, still grieved over Freddie and the family he'd left behind.

I pondered Mario's experience after he left therapy. Was he purposely drawn to that Irish village because there was an unfinished spiritual need for the part of him that was Freddie to grieve? I also understood that Mario needed to be believed. As he told me, "Thanks for taking me seriously. It's not the first time I've told this story but I never felt believed." It was obvious that Mario's happening upon this village was the environmental trigger that brought these memories to consciousness; memories Mario claimed as his own from a previous life. There was no reason for me to have doubted him.

To provide closure on this experience, I questioned Mario about what he thought he might do for Freddie. He decided to make a memorial to him out in the desert garden on his property. Such an action provided a sense of peace for Mario. He was believed.

My client, James, on the other hand, described a recurring "memory" or vision that suggested to me he was receiving someone else's experience because he was himself hypersensitive due to childhood trauma.

James was a young gay man who escaped to Las Vegas from the repressive and homophobic Deep South. He needed to explore who he was, and in doing so, met a young man named Harry. As Harry and James tried building a long-term relationship, they felt they were only bumbling along, unable to communicate much outside their bedroom, and with no idea how to establish goals and project them into the future as a couple. All the negative reinforcement and repression James had suffered in the South for being gay got in the way of a successful relationship. Harry suggested couples therapy and they unwisely chose a therapist associated with James' parents' church. Rather than working with the two men toward a successful relationship, the therapist told them to quit having sex because it was "against God's will." Filled with a sense of futility, James broke down, embarked on a three-week drinking binge and considered suicide. Harry brought him to see me, and I established a therapy program for James' personal issues.

What I learned was that James had been the victim of terrifying sexual abuse by his uncle who threatened to murder him if he told anyone what was happening. The uncle was a mortician who abused James in the same room where he prepared bodies for burial. With terror in his heart, James lived a silent childhood, feeling fearful most of the time. The covert threat of damnation as brought forward by the church therapist was the trigger that took James back to memories of his abusive uncle's threats of murder. I learned that odors like flowers, reminiscent of the mortuary, often caused James to have out-of-body experiences with long periods of amnesia. In trying to fill in those missing memories, at his request, I placed James into trance for regressive therapy. For about ten minutes we shared slow storytelling as some childhood memories came forward. But then James seemed to "go away" and I could no longer reach him. When I called him out of trance, much to my surprise, he awoke, gave me a wide-eyed look, and asked, "Who are you?" I then understood that he was suffering from dissociative identity disorder caused by his childhood trauma of sexual abuse.

While in therapy, from time to time, James described an experience that wasn't a dream or memory, but an ordered, organized vision that came to him when he was in the theta state between waking and sleeping. In this vision he was a child traveling on a bus in some forested wilderness. There was writing in front of him and what he described to me were characters of the Cyrillic alphabet– the bus may have been Russian. A blond-haired man sitting next to him was attending to him. "I think he was meant to be my father," James said. The two were seated behind the driver and James could see the lights from the bus spreading over a deserted highway. All of a sudden the bus vibrated and the other passengers began shouting. The vehicle went into what James described as a swerving motion, and then there was a sense of falling and a crashing sound. James explained that in his next memory, after that, he was floating above a tree-covered mountainside. That was the end of the memory.

The vision repeated itself over and over when he crossed through the theta state of consciousness. It was a real and detailed experience—but obviously not his own since James had been 18 years old the first time he went on a long bus trip and he could not speak or read Russian. It's possible James was remembering a past life of his own. But since I had determined that he was a dissociative, I wondered whether James was experiencing an opening between dimensions where he was reliving the memories of another entity who was "floating around" and had the traumatic experience that James witnessed through his vision. Was it James' consciousness that gave this spirit with unfinished business an opportunity to understand what had happened or was it his own spiritual presence in another life?

Such memories leak out in the strangest ways. Mary sought my help when she became a widow at a very young age and not only had grief issues, but needed to find ways to go on with life. We were making good progress in her therapy when she asked, "Maybe you can help me with something? I've been having this dream for years and it keeps going on and on. I wonder if it's trying to give me some special message."

The dream took place in what Mary thought was a city in Europe with very old architecture and cobble stone streets. "I know that the person having the experience in the dream is me," Mary said. "Sometimes I'm the one who's participating and sometimes I seem to be watching from outside of me." She saw herself as a teenage girl in a formal green dress, standing on the balcony of one of the old buildings. "In the very last moment," Mary remembered, "I'm watching myself from above. I'm looking out over a classic cityscape of quaint old buildings and all of a sudden a big explosion shoots up from under the building. That's the last thing I remember and I keep dreaming it over and over!"

Mary's dream, like James' vision and Mario's past-life memory, are visions of tragic, out-of-the-blue experiences that end human lives.

Abrupt, life-stealing moments are being re-lived by beings of a future time, and suggesting unfinished business about feelings at that last-moment event.

"What if that really was you in a former life?" I asked Mary. "What comes to mind about that last moment?"

"I was just another innocent being living my life and minding my own business when I was caught in the crosshairs of men who know how to do nothing but make war and kill people!" Mary said as she wiped a few tears away.

"If you could send a message back to this innocent that was standing on a balcony, what would you tell her?"

"I would tell her not to despair," Mary said. "There's another life waiting with beautiful children, grandchildren, a husband that loves, and many nice experiences." Having made this peace with her prior self, Mary's dreams stopped.

A similar dream plagued my client, Mark.

"I'm in Europe," he remembered, "because people are speaking some Eastern European language. In the dream I seem to understand what they're saying. I don't know the language myself, but I know the sounds. I'm with a small group of people and one man seems to be the spokesperson or leader. We're all crouched up against the wall of an empty train station. I can see rows of benches that look like church pews and ticketing windows. The man is both talking and gesturing. He seems to be telling us to stay low against the wall. It sounds like thunder outside. All of a sudden there's this big flash and that's the end of the dream. It's mystified me since I was a teenager and I don't know what to make of it."

Mark extended the question of whether I believed in reincarnation. But I also told him there's a lot of "stuff" floating around in the ether and perhaps we have the ability to "pick up on it" or maybe it just "seeps" into our consciousness. Mark was receptive to both theories, but I thought it important to ask him what meanings and feelings were woven through the images for him.

"It was obviously war, and war is terrible!" he said. "So many innocent people suffer because of it. If humanity is going to grow philosophically, we must stop war. It gets in the way of everything we could be!"

When I asked what he would say to the "self" in his dream that evidently experienced sudden death, Mark said, "I would tell him that it seems like life is over, but it really isn't. There will be other times and other places where all of us can have a voice in making change happen. We won't have to spend our lives crouched in train stations waiting for a bomb!" Several months later Mark came back for a tune-up for managing his anxieties. After our discussion of his dream he had written letters to elected Federal officials regarding U.S. involvement in the Middle Eastern wars. Having had his say on such issues brought some resolution and his dream never returned.

After having a multitude of such experiences with the patient population that frequents my little one-man therapy office, I came to the conclusion that many people have such stories to tell. It's my sincere wish that they share their spiritual journeys and the messages that accompany them with the world. They could be the harbingers of change for the planet.

* * *

TWELVE

*"Synchronicity is an ever present reality for
those who have eyes to see." Carl Jung*

Synchronicity

In the 1990's our country was in the midst of a culture war (not that it
still isn't), and emotions ran high. This was during the worst part of the
AIDS epidemic and many portions of our community were freaking out.
Not only was there major hysteria over HIV, but many individuals in
healthcare had never seen a gay couple and just didn't know how to handle
that or what to make of it, but we could no longer live under the radar. So
I spread myself around offering information and a lecture regarding the
bio-genetics of sexual orientation regarding what was known at the time.
I was lecturing to a graduate-level behavioral health class when I noticed
a young man whose body language and facial expression reflected anger.
He finally pointed his finger at me and said, *"You're going to hell!"*

"Here we go, off and runnin" I thought. I reminded him calmly, "There
are many different beliefs and you are certainly entitled to yours. We're
here today to examine many different viewpoints and mine happens to be
science and research-based." The man remained quiet but still obviously
angry. Later I complained to the program director that if that student took
his prejudices into the professional world, he could cause a great deal of
damage to vulnerable people. This incident remained in the back of my
mind and always troubled me along with a myriad of similar others.

The years passed and as a patron of the Las Vegas community I engaged
in a great deal of movement around our bustling city. I was in and out
of many favorite businesses and restaurants populated by pleasant staff

and customers. I came to know many people in various establishments by name, and always introduced myself and passed on a business card. A favorite waiter in a neighborhood restaurant was a man named George.

As I patronized George's place of employment, one day he announced that he had a friend in Phoenix that wished to confer with me and wanted to know if he could pass my phone number along. I encouraged the contact and a few days later I took a call from George's friend. "Hi Ron," he said. "It's Calvin. Remember me? I'm the guy from that class years ago who told you that you were going to hell. I just wanted you to know that I support you and your wonderful spirit. The remarks I made that day were all about the church that I belonged to, and those beliefs went away a long time ago."

I was stunned. That moment eighteen years prior that had so irritated me was now resolved for both Calvin and me in the most positive manner. All I did was frequent businesses; if I had chosen a different restaurant; or if I had not met George, I would not have had that bridge to the past. How many restaurants are there in "The Entertainment Capital of the World" and how many Georges are there? What were the chances of such a thing happening? But it did happen and the result was resolution of a difficult and irritating incident in my life. The event represented "the icing on the cake" of a massive cultural change and threw a little water on the fires of a culture war.

This is synchronicity.

Carl Jung described synchronicity as the manifestation of meaningful coincidences. It's about when the chances of a significant event occurring are normally about a million to one—but synchronous events happen in close proximity to each other. Jung insisted that awareness of synchronicities is a sign of spiritual awakening. Michael Talbot, in his book, *The Holographic Universe*, comments in detail regarding Jung's beliefs and his experience with synchronicity [16]:

> Jung encountered many such meaningful coincidences
> during his psychotherapeutic work and noticed that
> they almost always accompanied periods of emotional

intensity and transformation: fundamental changes in belief, sudden and new insights, deaths, births, even changes in profession. He also noticed that they tended to peak when the new realization or insight was just about to surface in a person's consciousness. As [Jung's] ideas became more widely known, other therapists began reporting their own experiences with synchronicity. Because of their striking nature, Jung became convinced that such synchronicities were not chance occurrences, but were, in fact, related to the psychological processes of the individuals who experienced them. Since he could not conceive of how an experience deep in the psyche could cause an event or series of events in the physical world ... he proposed that some new principle must be involved, an acausal connecting principle hitherto unknown to science.

Many people can point to synchronistic events in their life, born from the emotional intensity Jung describes, and I've had many in my own.

I went to graduate school in the Los Angeles area at a time when thousands of people were dying of AIDS. I was working full time and carrying a heavy course load at school. In addition, because I had escaped the epidemic and was in good health, I resolved to do what I could to make the situation better for those who were suffering. I wasn't sure how I could do that and the internal argument was very intense and emotional for me. And trying to keep up with my full-time job and full-time class work put me under tremendous strain.

Every other week there was a psycho-social briefing on AIDS at UCLA's Neuro-Psychiatric Institute which I made a point to attend. I should have been home writing term papers but I also needed to be at those briefings to learn what I could about how to help with the AIDS epidemic. Two of my personal missions were in competition with each other and my emotional stress was overwhelming. During one of these briefings I sat next to an psychologist named Daniel and we struck up a conversation.

I explained my dilemma, complained that I ought to have been home writing my term paper on cross-cultural issues, but needed to be at this briefing, too. It just so happened (meaningful coincidence) that Daniel taught cross-cultural issues at UCLA. "Let me give you a hand," he said, "and at least save you a trip to the library." Daniel gave me an audio cassette recording of his class on Asian cultures, and from his briefcase handed me several cross-cultural studies I could use to write my term paper. With Daniel's help, I was able to not only relax and gain information from the briefing, but completed the term paper for my graduate studies as well. I found the coincidence remarkable: what chance was there that of the hundreds of people in the auditorium that day I should have chosen to sit next to the one person most able to help me and, in doing so, relieve me of the emotional stress I was going through in trying to balance conflicting goals?

As Jung pointed out, mental and emotional stress very often give rise to synchronistic events.

When I returned to Las Vegas after finishing graduate school and opened a non-profit treatment agency, finding adequate funding to treat our patient population caused me tremendous anguish. Our budget for AIDS care at that time was only $90,000—and we were treating ninety AIDS patients alone in addition to many others with serious mental and emotional needs. At one point we lost that $90,000 to another agency and were advised by the funding source to simply let our ninety HIV-positive patients go. It was ghastly and heartless advice and I lost a good deal of sleep wondering what I could do to save our AIDS program and our patients. We had deep therapeutic relationships with these patients that were important and respectful. Aware of our dilemma, a friend of the agency loaned us the $90,000 we'd lost so we could continue our work. I signed a promissory note to repay the loan, but with no idea of how I would be able to do so. I was working on blind faith that the situation would resolve itself.

And so it did. The agency's insurance company sent a letter. I wondered at first whether we'd missed a payment even though I was certain we'd been faithful in making our payments for several years. What the letter informed, however, was that the insurance company was going public and how did we want the $180,000 we'd invested to be refunded—in stock or cash? We now had twice the $90,000 we had needed to keep the AIDS program going. I felt a profound sense of Spirit woven through this synchronistic event: the energy created by my own anguish and concern, as well as the agency's unconditional commitment to our patients manifested a resolution.

Yet another synchronistic event had deeply personal meaning for me because it involved death and the promise of spirit living on afterward.

My dear friend Jerry died of AIDS on April 18, 1994. He had a definite style and way of thinking about himself that he often shared with me. He wore a paisley bandana, plaid shirts, and medium-colored blue jeans. He wore a large pair of sunglasses against the harsh Nevada sun and many times told me, "I think I have more of a female spirit than male!" He always carried a paperback book and cherished Bonnie, his cockapoo, who followed him everywhere and was very affectionate.

In the days following Jerry's death, I was overwhelmed by the loss of my friend and buried myself and my grief in my work.

I'd gone into the agency on a Sunday afternoon to catch up on work I had neglected during the week. The commercial neighborhood where we were located was deserted. Because any residential areas were quite a distance away, it was unlikely anyone would wander into the business complex. And yet ....

Sitting at my desk I saw a cockapoo come up to my office window—it was the perfect image of Jerry's dog, Bonnie. My heart jumped. I went outside and the dog approached me so I could pet her, just as I had often petted Bonnie. I heard a voice in the distance say, "Isn't she adorable? This little girl is the joy of my life!" A young woman was approaching and her appearance shocked me. She wore a paisley bandana and a pair of large sunglasses. She was clad in a plaid blouse and denim skirt that went down to her ankles with a paperback book in one hand. By now, I fully grasped the power and meaning of what I saw. I could feel my heart pounding!

"Do you live in the neighborhood?" I asked.

"I'm always in the neighborhood," she said with a smile. I expected she'd say, "Yes, over on Sixth Street," and what was she doing in this deserted commercial area that was the home of frequent drug deals? I was mystified. "Working on Sunday?" she questioned in a familiar way, almost as if she knew me.

"Oh, just getting caught up," was my answer.

She attached a leash to the dog's collar. "Well, you take care now." She walked away down the sidewalk and disappeared. In the following weeks I looked for the woman and her dog but I never saw them again. Whatever type of synchronistic event this was, I took its meaning that a dear friend whom I loved deeply wanted to let me know he was all right and still around.

Noting the synchronicities in my own life, I was able to recognize and point them out in the lives of my clients, as well, and help them to see the power and personal meaning of such events.

Julie suffered a form of obsessive-compulsive disorder that drove her to sit for hours in a bedroom chair ruminating on philosophical questions with no answers, such as "Is there a God?" Or, "Am I good person?" The disorder had reached such a pitch that she was determined to be disabled and unemployable. Julie's husband, Jack, loved her deeply, but the disorder was taking a serious toll on their marriage. Faced with the potential loss of this loving relationship, Julie pushed herself into therapy.

I approached her intervention from the perspective of "utilization," a healing process named by psychiatrist, Milton Erickson, who believed that we all have the internal tools and qualities we need to cope, make changes, and transcend life's barriers. In Julie's case, in hypnosis, I substituted the dark, somewhat unresolvable nature of her obsessions with lighter scenes and subjects that were built around her favorite color—green–to mitigate her underlying depression. While in trance, I guided her in walks past green pine-treed mountains and green rivers and suggested an atmosphere of joy and pleasure. I also added my own symbolism to Julie's trances in the form of a white healing dove that would fly through the sky or land on an imaginary tree limb. I suggested that the dove, as a symbol of hope, which I used often, would provide her with empowering and encouraging messages telepathically.

The process worked. I countered the obsessions with artful, healing landscapes and experiences. Julies sense of imagination had been jump started. I gave her audio tapes of the trance work to take home. Julie's nature and attitude lightened and she drew pictures of the imaginary images she saw when pondering the suggestions I'd provided. The white dove was always in her drawings, and she began to see the light at the end of the tunnel. She came to truly understand that she had "choice" in what she allowed into her head space.

One day Julie arrived for therapy particularly excited.

"It's here," she said. "It's really here!"

"What's here?"

"The white dove!" she said. Julie and Jack had been in their garden when a white dove flew through and sat on a nearby tree limb. Julie put her finger out and the dove came up to meet it. "It came to me and I'm well!" Julie was recovered, ceased her obsessive ponderings, secured employment, and became an equal partner in her loving relationship with Jack.

As for the dove, I wondered whether Julie had focused so intently on it that her torsion field energy and consciousness crossed the boundary between this dimension and the next and manifested the dove as a synchronistic event reinforcing the promise of a better future that her therapeutic dove represented.

Sometimes when I'm called upon for therapy I struggle to create an effective treatment program for a given client based upon their particular set of problems and challenges. One afternoon I had a telephone call from a person named Arthur requesting an appointment that I really did not want to make because I was at my max in every aspect of managing the agency and my case load. "I really need some help in understanding what's going on with me," he said. The desperation in his voice persuaded me, and I made an appointment for him the following Monday morning. That Sunday evening I watched a news story about individuals who had received polio inoculations when in elementary school and developed post-polio syndrome as adults. The report suggested that many persons, who received the inoculations, although they may have never developed a full-blown version of polio, had developed physical problems in later adulthood. Arthur came into my office feeling anxious and depressed because his legs seemed to be twisting involuntarily and no one seemed to be able to tell him what was wrong. There had been many theories, but no real answers.

Where I might otherwise have been at a loss for theories and suggestions for Arthur, had I not seen the previous night's news program, in that synchronistic way, I may not have had any ideas for Arthur. I explained to him that we could work on his depression and anxiety, but since I did not practice medicine I was just another person that could not help him with his physical issues. Having suspicions, however, I asked him if he had been inoculated for polio while in elementary school. With his affirmative answer, I suggested that he watch the program from the night before. It's as though the anguish of this man drifted out through the spiritual ether to produce the information I needed to set the direction for his therapy and referrals. As it came to be, his physician diagnosed him with post-polio syndrome. He now wears braces on his legs and he's moving around quite well. How much more obvious, as Carl Jung would say, can the meaningful coincidence be?

In his book *The Road of Time*[17], French physicist Phillipe Guillemant suggests that the future has already happened and emerges from how we presently see events and what we intend to do in the future. He theorizes that our intentions cause effects in the future that become "future causes of present effects" which he identifies as synchronicities. We simply need to incorporate this concept into our awareness in order to see the phenomenon. We can recognize weak signals in the present that tell us what is about to emerge.

Many of my patients who have had out-of-body experiences and whose consciousness has crossed into the next dimension have all made the same observation. In that place, they relate that the past, present, and future exist simultaneously. I believe that when our emotions are more intense it makes our torsion field more active. It's the torsion field that can penetrate the veil between this dimension and the next and carry our consciousness, its intentions and observations, along with it. This energy touches that version of the future that most coincides with our intentions and presents something meaningful to us in the emerging present.

When I was emotionally torn over the conflict between my need to attend AIDS lectures and my need to accomplish my assignments in graduate school, a resolution appeared: Daniel, the cross-cultural psychologist. In the incident of the woman outside my office with her little cockapoo, my emotions after Jerry's death were raw. My thoughts, intentions, and observations relative to Jerry's death "tickled" the future to produce the synchronistic experience I needed to assuage my grief.

Another thing my dissociative clients have told me is that when they travel out-of-body and experience the next dimension, there are no questions in that place. Everything is known. Several of my patients explained that when out-of-body and in an altered state, they would no sooner think of a question than the answer appears in thoughts immediately. It's no surprise that some of our greatest minds like Albert Einstein, Leonardo Da Vinci, and Nikola Tesla all had meditative practices which helped their intentions to materialize in wondrous ways and discoveries. Their deep desire to solve their questions and intentions excited their torsion fields and sent them to the place where all answers exist. Wishes reallydo have power! Our consciousness change the world!

Synchronicity

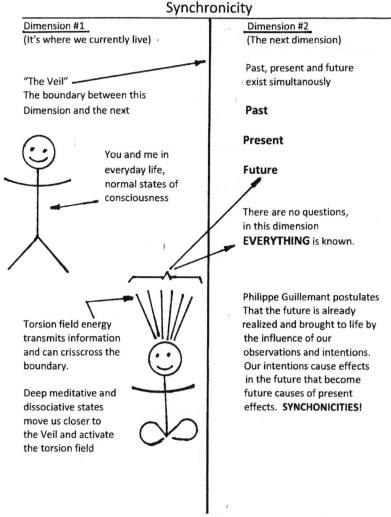

Dimension #1
(It's where we currently live)

"The Veil"
The boundary between this
Dimension and the next

You and me in
everyday life,
normal states of
consciousness

Torsion field energy
transmits information
and can crisscross the
boundary.

Deep meditative and
dissociative states
move us closer to
the Veil and activate
the torsion field

Dimension #2
(The next dimension)

Past, present and future
exist simultanously

Past

Present

Future

There are no questions,
in this dimension
EVERYTHING is known.

Philippe Guillemant postulates
That the future is already
realized and brought to life by
the influence of our
observations and intentions.
Our intentions cause effects
in the future that become
future causes of present
effects. **SYNCHONICITIES!**

Figure 3 indicates how synchronicity may occur from a theoretical perspective.
Taken into account here is the theory of Philippe Guillemant who postulates
the physics of information and self-reports of dissociative patients who have
trans-dimensional experiences. It's a place where science and spirit meet!

* * *

THIRTEEN

"Two possibilities exist: either we are alone in the Universe or we are not. Both are equally terrifying." Arthur C. Clarke

We Have Never Been Alone in the Universe

Walking into the beautiful art deco Memorial Theater in McKeesport, Pennsylvania was a joy. Built in 1926, the theater was a source of great entertainment for my father and me. On this particular day in 1952– wow! Flying saucers! I don't know which was bigger: the saucers on the screen or my own two eyes. It was "guys' afternoon out" and my dad had taken me to see the movie, *The Day the Earth Stood Still*, starring Patricia Neal and Michael Rennie.

On our way to see the movie Dad explained what flying saucers were believed to be, and he told me about the controversy over the UFO crash in Roswell, New Mexico that had happened just five years before. Dad said that, in his opinion, these were beings from other planets that came to visit and learn about us. Once the movie flickered onto the screen, I was fascinated.

The Day the Earth Stood Still tells the story of an interplanetary visitor, accompanied by a robot, who comes to Earth to deliver a warning. The visitor, Klaatu, played by Rennie, tells the world that we are toying dangerously with atomic energy and weapons. He warns that if we are going to save the Earth and minimize problems in our planetary neighborhood we'd better knock it off.

For a long time our culture, assisted by government debunkers, ridiculed people who believed that UFOs were real. But this attitude has begun changing and the subject of UFOs is being taken more seriously. Respectable individuals such as the former governor of Arizona, Fife Symington, have come forward to testify regarding their UFO sightings. In Governor Symington's case, he noted his personal sighting of "The Phoenix Lights" which was witnessed by thousands of people in the skies over Phoenix, Arizona in 1997. Former presidents Jimmy Carter and Ronald Reagan each spoke of personal sightings and were certainly believers. President Reagan even mentioned in a speech to the United Nations the possibility of hostile aliens, which is partly why he proposed his Star Wars defense initiative. Prior to his death in 1995, Ben Rich, co-founder of Lockheed-Martin's Skunk Works advanced development programs, made two profound statements about the truth of UFOs. First, he said, "We now have the technology to take ET home." Then he added, "There are the UFOs that we build and the UFOs built by them [extraterrestrials]." On October 9th, 2014, former NASA Chief, Charles Bolden, in an interview on UK TV, said, "Mars is the most likely planet in our solar system that had life at one time and may have life now." Even esteemed astronaut, Edgar Mitchell, confirmed the existence of extraterrestrials before he died.

The point of all these statements is that we are not alone in the universe and likely never were. It's believed that there are one hundred billion galaxies in the universe. Imagine the possibilities for finding life among them!

What does this mean to me as a psychotherapist? My fellow professionals often provide trauma recovery services to individuals who claim to have been abducted by extraterrestrials. I've had professional experience with abductees–although this information first came to me in an unexpected way.

My spouse, Daniel, and I long enjoyed the company of our friend, David, who lived in Palm Springs, California. David and Daniel had been friends since college; David was also a widower whose spouse, Douglas, had died of AIDS and David himself was HIV-positive. Daniel and I made frequent trips to Palm Springs from Las Vegas to spend time with David. One particular time we arrived and found David lying across his bed unconscious, barely alive. We got him to the hospital; tests revealed one of the side effects of his HIV medication was diabetes. Treated and regulated, David was out of the hospital the next day.

As we drove him home David said "That really was a close call and if it wasn't for the two of you, I would have been dead. Experiences like this help us understand that our time on Earth is limited and I think it's important to share something with the two of you, something I've never told anyone." Once we had David home and settled, I curiously asked, "Well, what is it you want to tell us?"

"I want you both to know that I'm not crazy," David said. How many times have I heard this from patients about to say something unusual? "It's like this," David went on. "I was abducted by aliens." This was the first time I'd heard this from someone I knew and I was shocked. "Don't worry," David assured us. "I'm okay. Obviously, I lived through it."

David remembered at least seven abduction experiences, starting when he was ten years old. He wandered away from friends in a park and suddenly found himself in a room being examined by a blond man in a uniform. "He was very kind and loving," David said, "And now I understand I was inside a ship of some kind. But the next thing I knew I was back outside standing in the park." When he later asked his mother when he could go "back to that hospital" where the doctor was so nice and wore a funny uniform, his mother told him he hadn't been in a hospital since he was born. David recalled other abduction experiences as he grew up—always examined by the same compassionate blond man, never frightening, and communicating telepathically. Sometimes, David said, there were other people on the ship having the same experience. "On several occasions, before they dismissed us back to our environments, they took us into a big room where one whole wall was like a movie screen. They showed us pictures of destruction and devastation and told us that we must relate to our leaders that they must prevent such things from happening. The next thing I knew, I'd be back where I was previously." David also noted that one wall of the ship was transparent and he could see through it to the landscape outside. He had been taken from many different environments: a plateau in a mining area in Arizona, and driving at night on U. S. 95 from Las Vegas to Reno to name a couple.

David further described having no memory of how he'd gotten from the ship back to the place where he'd been abducted. His examinations often included skin scraping, drawing blood and fluids from his body—and one time he found an implant. "I found a small, long piece of metal under the skin of my left upper arm," he said. "My doctor made an incision and pulled it out with tweezers. We put it in a jar and I planned to take it over to the lab at White Sands. But when I got up the next morning, it had turned to dust."

"Can you discuss the last time you were abducted?" I asked.

"Oh yes. I was up in the Russian River area in Northern California," David said. "Douglas was over in Bodega Bay, and I was on my way to meet him. At that time, neither one of us knew that we were infected with HIV. On my way to get Doug, I was taken one more time. It was made known to me by the blond man that I wouldn't be taken again and he telepathically said goodbye. Sometimes I wonder if he had the power to make me well. If he did, why didn't he? But then, I was being studied, wasn't I?"

I asked David what he felt these experiences meant for him.

"There must be a whole universe full of life out there," he answered. "And it's time this world started knowing that and that those in the know start telling the truth. We need to change our very paradigm of existence and adjust our thoughts and beliefs to a much bigger picture."

David later died of AIDS, but his story was not the last I would hear of extraterrestrial abduction. Another experience that was related to me was in a professional context and was completely different from David's.

Pearl, one of the staff therapists at our agency, asked me to join her in a session with a patient. She had been treating a man using hypnosis as a tool. He wanted to retrieve memories and bring the jigsaw puzzle of his life together. "What is this thing of being abducted by aliens?" Pearl asked. "I've never had a case like this before and I need your help." I went into the session and watched Pearl facilitate a trance induction for the patient named Alan.

Alan described creatures with trans-dimensional abilities that intruded into his bedroom one night by walking through the walls. He woke up on an examining table surrounded by these creatures who "poked, prodded and stuck [him] with needles." Even in trance, it was obvious as the memories unfolded that Alan was terrified. He shook and cried. He saw other people there who were suffering the same experience. He said that, "Even though no movement was felt by me or the others, the vehicle was soon on the ground." A large door opened into a barren desert environment where Alan and the others lined up to leave. No one spoke, and from what Alan remembered and perceived, it appeared that he and the others were in shock. They were escorted onto a second vehicle and the next thing Alan remembered is that he was back in bed. His pajamas were unbuttoned and in disarray and strange images of his experience drifted through his mind. He wondered if he'd been harmed physically as there were places on his body that were sore. Two months after this experience, Alan was in therapy with Pearl wanting to know what his haunting dreams and images were all about. When Pearl had drawn his memory out through hypnosis, Alan was angry, outraged, and terrified that such things could happen against one's will. Pearl spent weeks creating space for Alan to process, understand his experience, and recover emotionally. Obviously, the pleasant, compassionate visitor that came to my friend David was not the only kind that was abducting human beings.

Both David and Alan were people of tremendous integrity. I believe their experiences were real and until they described them to me, I considered the whole extraterrestrial matter to be part of the world of conspiracy theory and fantasy. But motivated by their experiences and others whose stories I've heard, I've changed my mind. Knowing that we are not alone in the universe gives me a sense of anticipation and hope that this truth might become more widely known during my lifetime and benefit humanity in some way. Perhaps such knowledge will turn our attention to the cosmos instead of engaging in earth-bound squabbles. Yet another part of me is afraid to know that just like Earth, the universe is seasoned with both good and evil. Finally, it angers me that the truth, as expressed through the experiences of David, Alan, and many others, is being kept from us by such institutions as government and religion who have vested interests in maintaining control of populations in our present paradigm of existence. Looking beyond the Earth would definitely change the paradigm. It might make some of the powers-that-be matter a whole lot less!

But disclosure by the people and institutions who take charge on this Earth will come. With so much information about extraterrestrials available on the Internet, in the media, and through first-hand accounts of abductees and others who have experienced some form of contact with them, the truth is becoming much more difficult to deny and hide. When disclosure happens, there will be three kinds of reactions. And those of us in the therapeutic helping professions may be needed to assist in helping others to manage their conceptions and feelings.

First, there will be a whole segment of the public that says, "Ho hum. We knew it all along. Anything else you want to tell us?"

Another part of the public will experience what we call cognitive dissonance where they will be faced with two competing sets of facts they need to reconcile. These people have created and lived within a certain worldview their whole lives and have certain beliefs for how life works and how they fit into it. Disclosure of the existence of extraterrestrial life will challenge their paradigm. They will need to reconcile their beliefs with this new information and their worldview will be shaken. They will need to engage directly with a process of reconciliation which will be very difficult for them to work through and they will likely need therapeutic intervention and help.

There will also be a third set of the population which, upon learning the truth of extraterrestrial life, will go into emotional shock. These people have been isolated in their own specific belief systems and resist change. They will refuse, at first, to engage in the psychological process that would help them integrate new information into their belief system. Their denial will manifest in protest, anger, and perhaps violence against themselves or others. These people may require months of therapy to help them grieve their loss of "old ways," to accept eventually the reality of extraterrestrials, and to redefine their place not only in the world but in the universe.

But once our consciousness has changed and we've incorporated the knowledge that we are surrounded by life in the universe, we will develop a sense of expanding adventure as well as anticipation and hope for a better future than we seem to be facing now.

* * *

FOURTEEN

"Empaths did not come into this world to be victims, we came to be warriors. Be brave. Stay strong. We need all hands on deck." Anthon St. Maarten

Psychic Sensitivity and Empathy in Children

Children are remarkably sensitive to unusual phenomena. They often experience and say things that adults around them find strange and inexplicable; things usually attributed to childish imagination. But what we call childish imagination may in fact be children's close interaction with other dimensions.

One day my friend, Laura, described an unusual conversation she had experienced with her four-year-old daughter.

"She was getting dressed one morning and she asked me if I had her sash," Laura said. "Neither I nor anyone in my family has ever used that word. I asked her what she meant by the word *sash* and she made a gesture on the front of her dress. I knew that it meant a frontal decoration—but it was a word that hadn't been used in our home or anywhere my daughter may have gone. When I asked her where she heard the word, she said that it was what we wore before. How does such a thing happen?"

I was mystified at the time and had no explanation. My response was rather flimsy. "Sometimes," I said, "words and facts just seem to float around in the ether and maybe we're a bit like antennas and pick up on them."

Susan, one of my patients [whom I mention with more detail in Chapter 5], was very specific after her automobile accident when she told her parents which of her grandparents would die first and which would be last. Her parents told her that they'd rather not know such things and Susan thereafter kept her psychic gift to herself. It wasn't until she came into therapy that I helped her understand the nature of her psychic change since her out-of-body experience.

Another friend, Patricia, remarked that many times she had watched young children in play activities. She was astounded when she saw one of them stop playing, pause, and then come up with some profound remark. "I always wondered where those behaviors come from. It's as though they're acquiring information from somewhere outside of themselves," she remarked.

Because of stories like Laura's, Susan's, and Patricia's, I've come to believe that sometimes children make statements to their parents based on information they acquire from the next dimension. Because this information is usually not in the parents' context or frame of reference, it's either misunderstood or ignored, and the child may be ridiculed or chastised.

It has been established that from birth to seven years old children live in the theta brain wave state, which is the dream-like place between waking and sleeping. It's where we go during hypnosis, and in my opinion, this state moves us closer to the veil between this dimension and the next where the past present and future exist simultaneously, and where all knowledge exists in the Akashic Record. Information regarding past lives may be found there, spirits may exist there, and the consciousness of those who have passed on may be present there.

I believe that since children live in the theta state of consciousness they are much more likely to experience "leaks" from the next dimension that may be random or purposeful. Laura's daughter, for example, may have used the unfamiliar word *sash* in a past life and unintentionally remembered it in her present life. Susan may have acquired her accurate knowledge of the death of her grandparents from the other side where past, present, and future exist together. And Patricia's observation may have been about some profound messages coming from the next dimension as reflected through children.

I know that I lived my own childhood closer to the veil and I remember several incidents.

When I was in third grade my teacher, Mrs. James, always ended the school week with a classroom game whose winner was given a chocolate candy bar. Once such game was *Pin the Tail on the Donkey*. No one loved chocolate more than I did. When it was my turn, Mrs. James fastened the blindfold firmly over my eyes then turned me loose to find the donkey after twirling me around a few times. Within a few seconds, however, the blackness I saw behind the blindfold transformed into a hazy view of the school room and the cardboard donkey—I went straight forward and pinned the tail, amazing both the class and Mrs. James. In a confused way Mrs. James remarked, "I know I had that blindfold firmly over your eyes!" Fiercely motivated by my love for chocolate, I know that I dissociated and my consciousness moved outside of my body to perform this daunting task. Obviously, I could dissociate at will during that time, but unfortunately can't do it in the present.

Another experience when I was in fourth grade convinces me that I was drawing upon knowledge and skills from beyond the veil that I did not ordinarily possess, just as Mozart expressed a highly developed musical skill from the time he was just three years old. My teacher, Mrs. Jones, passed around large sheets of paper and instructed us to draw whatever came to mind. Thinking of the Tarzan movies I enjoyed, I drew a leopard in a tree. It was a remarkably detailed and life-like picture that I could not duplicate if I were to try it today as an adult. My family claimed it to be museum material. I'm convinced that the temporary artistic talent came from the other side and just as quickly left me.

In general, children are not encouraged to understand, accept, or explore such experiences. Modern education too often instead encourages rote learning to pass standardized tests while discouraging challenge, curiosity, and abstract thought processes that can lead to psychic experience. In an article from *The Llewellyn Journal*, Sara Wiseman[18] lists several abilities and traits in children to watch for that may indicate a child has psychic abilities which should be freely explored:

1. Is your child highly sensitive or gifted?

2. Is he imaginative, creative or a right-brain thinker?

3. Does your child get the "vibe" of people and situations, even total strangers?

4. Is she affected by crowds or noisy places?

5. Does she sometimes say that she's been to a place before, even though you know she hasn't?

6. Does he have an imaginary playmate or say he hears voices?

7. Does she have a deep knowledge of her ancestors and you're not sure how?

8. Does he say that he sees ghosts?

9. Does she experience noises, flashes of light or other unexplainable occurrences?

10. Is your child deeply attracted to animals and has a special way of relating to them?

11. Does she have an urge to put her hands on things and help heal them?

12. Does your child see auras?

13. Does she have especially vivid dreams?

14. Does she understand the teachings of Jesus, Buddha or other Holy Ones and you are unsure of how this came to be?

I was especially fascinated with Wiseman's view that a child's imaginary playmate can also indicate psychic ability because it resurrected a memory I had long buried from the time I was three or four years old. My imaginary, or perhaps even spiritual playmate, came to me in the place between waking and sleeping, a deep theta state of consciousness. When my mother laid me down to sleep at night, as I drifted into slumber, I often found myself, at first, in an environment of complete blackness with no sense of containment. It was a warm place and not at all frightening. I always found there a small, elf-like being, alive and animated. We never shared dialogue but it was clear through his body language that he was overjoyed to see me. There was a light over the being and he wore a coat designed with a maze of shimmering, rainbow-colored rectangles, with a hat to match. After visiting this joyful little being, I'd drift on to sleep. Because I did not, at that age, have the verbal skills to describe my experience, I didn't have the ability to share it with my parents. As I reflect on this event, I feel that there is no way that such a young child could have authored such a detailed experience in imagination. I now know that this ornate being came to me.

Today, I believe this experience to have been trans-dimensional, but my reach for explanation is still tentative. Because it occurred for only a few weeks at the specific age at which we begin developing our sexual and gender identity, I've wondered whether, with his rainbow outfit, the being I saw was a harbinger of my developing into a gay man. In the struggle for gay rights, in which I played a part, the rainbow flag was born as a symbol of our movement. Further, although there was certainly nothing erotic about our encounter, the being was a male who expressed great love for me and great joy when I would "show up." 'Just very interesting!

There's another possible explanation. It's proven that an unborn child can experience the emotional reflection of its parents from an epigenetics standpoint. While my mother was pregnant with me, World War II was raging through Europe, taking a terrible toll on family living both here and there. My father, while awaiting shipment to the European Front and far from my mother, developed a tumor on his pituitary gland and had to undergo a dangerous brain surgery in an Army hospital. He was sent home on medical discharge—but he was not the same man afterward that my mother had married. I was born the day after he came home. Could the family trauma I experienced in utero have contributed to my being a dissociative person and did this little creature that comforted me and gave me joy come to alleviate my own inherited trauma?

Very often dissociative children, living in the theta state of consciousness, and experiencing various psychic phenomena, are also highly empathic. It's because they can feel the feelings of others and share similar reactions. In an article from *Psychology Today*, Dr. Judith Orloff[19] names ten traits of empathic people:

1. Empaths are highly sensitive.

2. They absorb other people's emotions.

3. Many empaths are introverted.

4. They are highly intuitive.

5. They need alone time.

6. Empaths can become overwhelmed in intimate relationships.

7. They are targets for energy vampires.

8. They become replenished in nature.

9. Empaths have highly tuned senses.

10. They have huge hearts and sometimes give too much.

I feel that I truly am an empath, and the quality is sometimes reflected in the deep connection with those for whom I've provided psychotherapy. While my family and teachers did not recognize or encourage my dissociative experiences and my empathic nature, my suggestion for the parents of such children is that they watch and listen with an open mind. Spiritual realities do exist and they may present themselves. Be aware of empathic traits. If some statement from a child emerges that doesn't seem to fit our present reality, rather than dismiss it, explore it. Look for emerging talents that seem to appear from nowhere. They may form a path to the future. Pay attention if the child expresses knowledge that they can't have learned through ordinary means.

In short, nurture and encourage such children and help them develop into the spiritual, empathic and insightful beings they were meant to be.

* * *

FIFTEEN

"You may say I'm a dreamer, but I'm not the only one. I hope someday you'll join us. And the world will live as one." John Lennon

Hope

As my own and my patients' experiences have shown, there is much more to human existence than what we can see, feel and touch. Given that we possibly live in a multiverse where many universes may exist simultaneously we may occasionally glimpse other dimensions. Yet, affirmation of these trans-dimensional experiences are mostly missing from the conversation of everyday life in U. S. culture, and especially so in the therapeutic professions. When these experiences are shared, those who experience them are often shamed, ridiculed, marginalized, disbelieved and labeled as psychotic. My friend, Maritza, who is from Brazil, told me, "I don't understand this culture. In South America we talk about the spirit world all the time. For instance, people often visit an energy healer as an adjunct to surgery. We believe that expressing our spirituality contributes to our healing. I feel like we are living in a partial reality here."

I've had many discussions about this with my friend, therapist/healer John Relph. John points out that a level of separation from self as a result of trauma or some other action may *associate* us either closer to the next dimension or jolt us across the barrier right into it. Rather than saying this person suffers from a dissociative disorder we might instead more positively call it an *associative* experience. Without the word *disorder*, the healing process, or return to everyday states of consciousness after trauma sounds less overwhelming and more compassionate. Naming it an associative experience, I believe, would be a less stigmatizing description.

A good part of this stigmatization of alternative states of consciousness comes from the attitude of *some* oppressive organized religions. If it isn't their philosophy or experience, it simply isn't. Ironically, however, it's the practice of prayer, encouraged by organized religion, which can, in any context, contribute to a healing process. I look, for instance, at the Catholic practice of saying a series of prayers in conjunction with Rosary beads. In addition to the prayers, such a practice can create an alternative state of consciousness and a slight sense of separation from this reality. That alternative state of consciousness in and of itself can be very beneficial. One of my acquaintances made the rosary beads an integral part of her day and lived well into her nineties. States of calmness and stress reduction can promote longevity.

Religion and Prayer

Many of my patients who have had dissociative or trans-dimensional experiences ask me, "What about God? Is there one?"

Most religions of the world have been created around metaphors related to humanity: human figures, characters and dramas. These religious philosophies and thought systems, with their concept of a Higher Being who is responsible for what happens in the world evolved because mankind needed a way to focus on and conceptualize an "Infinite." The teachings of Jesus, Buddha and others reflect moral and philosophical imperatives about ways to live on this planet. Religion provides one way to find that Infinite–providing it doesn't also separate or raise barriers in the human family. I watched a news report one day about a hurricane that struck the southern United States. A woman being interviewed after the storm said, "Our neighbors down the street died but we survived because God was with us!" I wondered who could teach such a warped theology insinuating that God would favor some over others in the midst of a hurricane. And please; I doubt very much that the Higher Consciousness cares about who wins a football game!

Another flaw in the philosophy of *some* organized religions is that if we believe in God and attend church, some special reward will be given to us on Earth. We are depicted in scripture and elsewhere as existentially "special." Yet, a busload of people slid off a cliff in Portugal while on a religious pilgrimage. God did not save them because they were on a pilgrimage. And what about the thousands of young boys and girls who were molested by priests and bishops in the Catholic Church? God did not rush out of the clouds to protect them. We are placed on this Earth with free will and even freedom of movement. We are here to accomplish mastery of what it means to exist. Those phenomena have the power to take us in the direction of good or evil.

The flaws and inconsistencies in organized religion, however, do not imply there is no "Higher Being;" they only suggest that our understanding of the nature of that Being may be flawed. Rather than understand that this Being in the human sense of the word—God in the sky looking down on humankind and manipulating our lives like a puppet master—we should perhaps understand it more in the Native American sense as the Great Spirit, or, as I like to call it, The Source. Such terminologies imply latitude. The Source is part of our creation. It runs around us and through us. It's with us in life, death and hurricanes. It's also part of many other beings that live in the universe due to the fact that we are not alone. In my beliefs, God is not a white-bearded old man with a "sin book" sitting in front of him keeping a moment to moment log of our transgressions. WE get to process our lives when or after we pass.

Organized religions teach prayer as the way to communicate with and perhaps influence God to work in our behalf. But if one rejects belief in an old man god conceived in our image and accepts instead the concept of a Universal Source, then prayer still is also a way to connect with and engage the power of the Source. Prayer reflects intention. Deep intentions and desires can activate our torsion field, which in turn can "tickle" future possibilities in the next dimension to set up synchronicity and manifestation in the unfolding present as it occurs in the dimension in which we live. Prayers expressed in the imagery of desire—"viewing the completed outcome as we want it to be"–are the most powerful. If events in the unfolding present can be prompted by intention, which, in turn, can cross the veil and tap at a version of the future, then we have definable power over our destiny. We can give fate a nudge through the intention of prayer or meditation. I've always felt that it may not matter who or what one prays to, but that the imagery of hope or change is introduced, felt and projected into the ether.

In fact, if one chooses not to believe in a Great Spirit or Source, we can think of our meditative imagery and desires as part of the physics of information as theorized by Phillipe Guillemont in his book, The Road of Time, [see chapter twelve]. We can meditate, imagine a goal, and know that when we do that, it matters.

If individual prayer can nudge fate for the individual, group prayer and meditation may well create a group consciousness that can nudge fate through the Source for a far broader benefit. I once visited the Catholic Shrine of the Black Madonna in Czestochowa, Poland in the moment of afternoon mass when worshippers were deeply in prayer. There was complete uniformity of intention as they recited their prayers in unison. Such power, I thought! Having followed these wonderful people of my own heritage, I knew that it was "this power" of the human will, spirit and intention that helped to dissolve the iron curtain that had been put in place by authoritarian communists. I wondered what limitless possibilities could exist if all people of the planet engaged in such activities with positive intentions for humanity and for the Earth, utilizing our own deep consciousness as the tool. The power of group consciousness is the path to everything humankind could become, and, perhaps, is essential to our continued physical survival and spiritual evolution. That may require giving up our concept of a human-like Being that keeps track of everyone's sins for the more spiritual concept of a Universal Source in order to work toward a greater good for all.

And, the world will not change by manipulating national boundaries as the globalists keep attempting to facilitate. But they do such things for wealth and power. The only key to a survivable, goal-oriented planet is through human consciousness.

Meditation

For those uncomfortable with the religious connotation of prayer, meditation is an equally effective path for connecting with the Source or engaging the physics of information; however one wishes to conceptualize it. Deep meditation can bring us closer to the veil that provides dimensional separation and sometimes even cross it for brief periods of time. This activates our torsion field energy and gives the future a nudge to help change our present reality. In easing their anxiety and angst I have taught dozens of my patients how to meditate and the methods are quite simple.

Start with sitting comfortably and inviting all of the tension to pass from your body. Since we are the masters of our own mind/body we can simply ask the tension to leave our presence. Close your eyes and move away from the outside world. Allow your thoughts/consciousness to synchronize with your breathing: feel the movement of air in and out of your nostrils and the gentle movement of your chest as it moves up and down. Doing this provides a sense of rhythm that's hypnotic in nature.

A good beginning method to practice meditation and alternative states of consciousness is guided imagery. In this process we embark on an imaginary journey in our mind that comes as close to the reality of being in a soothing, comforting place as possible. Picture yourself in a place that represents calmness, safety and stability. Immerse yourself in the experience: smell the scents, feel the wind, hear the sounds that exist there. As you journey more deeply, you arrive at the state of consciousness that manifests theta brain waves, the place between waking and sleeping, in closer proximity to the veil. And while you are in a meditative state, do you have wishes for yourself and for the world? Guided meditations are also widely available over the Internet.

Another simple meditation method involves counting. With your inner voice, count from one to ten. Synchronize the counting with your breathing. Go slow. When you get to ten, start over. For my patients who have a problem staying focused, I suggest that with their mind's eye they imagine the numbers appearing on a black board as this usually helps.

Still another method is choosing some word that has meaning for you and saying it over and over with your inner voice. Words such as *peace, love, one,* as well as the meditative *ohm,* are all appropriate. Again, for individuals who have trouble with initial focus, imagine the word written on a blackboard and synchronize voicing the internal word with your inward and outward breathing. Meditating twice a day for twenty minutes at a time is most effective. But the truth is that even just moments spent in meditation are helpful.

Aside from relieving anxiety, deep meditation—like deep prayer—can bring us closer to the veil, which can be very helpful in everyday life. When I worked as a mechanical designer, my supervisor, Gary, and I were struggling with designs for the hydroelectric generators in Grand Coulee Dam on the Columbia River in the State of Washington. One design was particularly difficult and we strategized back and forth for more than two weeks. One morning Gary said to me, "I've got it!" And his solution worked. I asked him how he had found the answer and he told me, "I take long, warm showers, and this idea just popped into my head this morning!" His warm shower created an alternate meditative state of consciousness which brought him close to the veil where the answer he needed appeared to him. When struggling with a problem we have a choice. We can symbolically pound our heads against the wall as we anxiously search for answers, or we can go to the quiet place inside where creativity can emerge.

Not only can meditation connect with our torsion field to produce trans-dimensional experiences, it can provide positive physical effects, as well. This process, which can actually effect our DNA through epigenetics, is described eloquently in Dr. Bruce Lipton's book, *The Biology of Belief.*[20] In essence, the way that we perceive our environment creates specific body chemistry. Chemical messengers created by our perceptions find their way to receptors on the outside of our cells, which, in turn have an effect on how the genes in a cell behave. The once central dogma of biology which inferred rigidly that only genes controlled everything about the destiny of a human being is beginning to fade. What if we spend time each day imaging beauty and peace? What a great chemistry to send through our bodies. It may have the power to effect who we are!

In addition to its positive physical effects, deep meditation improves mental and emotional health. Depression, anxiety and attention deficit disorders have all demonstrated positive improvement over time when meditation is practiced.

I once facilitated a quick psychiatric assessment on a female patient named Sarah before assigning her to another therapist. In her sixties, she looked drawn and exhausted and decided to pursue therapy to deal with trauma caused by childhood abuse. Her therapy lasted a year. All the pain and anguish stored in her memories and in her body came to the surface and were processed with closure. Her traumatic memories had moved to a quieter place inside. She was taught meditative techniques to help contain her anxiety. After her therapy had finished, Sarah approached me and I was surprised by the improvement in her physical appearance. The lines in her face had become more subdued. Her body language and countenance were animated. She was confident and enthusiastic. I was convinced of the physical, mental, and emotional benefits of deep meditation and, of course, psychotherapy as well.

Meditating with good intentions, as Sarah had done, made a distinct difference in her individual life. But once we engage in meditation practice for ourselves, a next step would be to gather in groups and meditate with positive intention for humanity and for the Earth. We might have to change how we protect old beliefs and develop greater latitude in some way. We might have to change some of our boundaries. Here and there on the Earth, such meditative events are happening. May they grow larger!

In November 2016, physicist Stephen Hawking, speaking at the Oxford University Union, explained that with current threats to our existence, the Earth and humanity have about one thousand years of life left. Just as individuals may sicken and die from physical and emotional trauma, humankind could die as well from the collective effects of political brutality, greed, war, and environmental degradation. If an individual can be healed through the power of meditation with good intention, humankind might also be healed through the power of group meditation as we image change and preservation for the planet.

When we meditate in groups, we enter alternate states of consciousness together. In the event that the population of the world is somehow able to collectively practice alternate states of consciousness together, we can only imagine the benefits that could transpire. I believe that not only would we see an improved profile in studies of individual health in our society, but the transformative effects emanating from peaceful, goal-directed group consciousness could be staggering.

A resident of Poland taught me the words "padroze propaganda," meaning "traveling propaganda." He explained that sometimes in his country, in the oppressive past, the only safe way of communicating was by word of mouth. It was through this "traveling propaganda" that the desire for freedom and equality traveled like wildfire through the hearts, minds and consciousness of the people. This group consciousness was brandished like a weapon in the face of oppression and it traveled with the power of intention. Authoritarian communism could not win under these circumstances. After all, how many people could they really place in prison or send to the Gulag? In our own "traveling propaganda" about the spiritual power of prayer with intent or group meditation with a collective alternate consciousness nudging the future, humankind could heal itself, the planet, and survive beyond Stephen Hawking's one-thousand-year deadline.

Ronald W. Lawrence

The Hope

A few days ago I watched a broadcast on spirituality and religion. A group of individuals had divided themselves into three camps. One camp included true believers in a traditional God and the dogma of organized religion. A second camp consisted of atheist non-believers. The third camp was simply spiritual in its outlook and expressed its belief in the Source and/or consciousness. The true believers and non-believers were adamant in their positions. When one of the middle-of-the-road spiritual advocates spoke, however, both believers and non-believers stonewalled him and cut him off at the knees.

It's that black and white nature of human interaction that must be changed to achieve peace and preservation based upon higher consciousness.

I believe this revolution won't be fought with guns or nuclear weapons. It will be a revolution in consciousness. The remarkable associative experiences with other dimensions that have been part of mine and my patients' lives are happening to thousands of people around the world on a daily basis. I believe that our own trans-dimensional and spiritual power lies in further exploring these places in our own consciousness. When large numbers of humankind start moving in this direction, the experience, the reach beyond ourselves, will deepen and spread like "padroze propaganda." Believe me, the powers-that-be on this earth are not going to come forward and lead humanity into intentioned meditations to unify the Earth. It will have to come from us!

Imagine millions of people meditating daily then gathering to share insights, intuitions, synchronicities and the exponential rise in their own creativity. If the group consciousness in formerly oppressed countries could dissolve the walls of communist oppression, think of what it might do for our vulnerable planet. Such an effort would help us envision the trappings of our own personal and cultural evolution and bring us to the highest places of goodness, growth and preservation of humankind. New insights, synchronicities, creativity, and philosophical depth could ensue. We would gain control over preserving the Earth and take back our lives from those who encourage corporate slavery and endless war.

I often wonder what might be the catalyst for such a massive revolution in spirituality and consciousness. Would it be the emergence of a new Gandhi-like leader or a Martin Luther King that could transcend barriers and draw the whole world together in spirit and universal consciousness with succinct goals on which to meditate? Would this imagined leader pilot the world into an alternate associative state of consciousness and bring us all together for the sake of a powerful and healthy future through intention? I hope so.

Or will the fact that we are not alone in the universe be an inspiration for humankind to once and for all join together, move away from petty conflict, and look ahead to the stars and the universe with unified conscious intention?

Or will we wait until the Earth is at the brink of disaster before we realize that the present systems under which we live have done little to insure our survival, but instead have promoted division, separation and ransacking of the planet? Will we wait until we're on the brink of a major extinction-level event which would be too late? Some scientists feel that we are already there.

Rightfully so, when I go out into the community and talk about meditating our existence and the Earth into a healthier survival-based future I am often asked to *be specific*. Meditate and image on what? First we must begin to see ourselves as a planetary society. National boundaries, although they are still real, have started to lose their importance. Let the politicians continue to fight over them, but we're moving on. The Internet has manifested a planet with powerful electronic connection and communication. As we reach for the stars our own planetary identity becomes our reality. We must join the consciousness of humanity for the sake of everything that represents a greater good.

Meditate on what? Let your mind run wild. One thing that comes to my mind as it flies out of the blue is *children*. Every child born on this

Earth must come into this world with maximum opportunity. We must consciously reflect on how, how many, and under what circumstances children will be brought onto this earth with maximum opportunities for nurturance, growth and love. Currently we are in the midst of a world-wide epidemic of child abuse and neglect. We must alleviate the painful experience of such manifestations for children and, in turn, give the Earth and our species the opportunity for healing and survival. Children who arrive on this Earth with empowerment will be our future. Let's image that!

We have much work to do with our consciousness. How about a world without war and the death and suffering that go with it? The war makers are few, and citizens of the world are billions. What if no one was willing to pick up a gun to make the war profiteers richer? Image a world without hunger or pollution. How about a world without addiction and an existence where the trappings of mental health are a priority? Feel free. Add to the list. The fact is that where all of this manifests is from our own consciousness; our spirit in motion.

We're going to need very courageous people to lead this revolution in consciousness because they will be risking their own lives in doing so. The forces that keep humankind trapped in continuing negative cycles are very powerful. From time to time, Spirit appears in various ways, as reflected in all the stories I've told. It's as though it's there just waiting for the bigger and better event that could assist world-wide unification of consciousness and spirit, and lead humankind into perpetual peace and preservation of the planet. May we choose to engage with that possibility through the power of our consciousness and spirit!

* * *

EPILOGUE

It was a peaceful Thursday morning. I could hear Dan up and about down on the first floor. I was lying on my side facing outward from the bed toward the western wall of the bedroom. I was just in that place between waking and sleeping and began to rouse, my eyes barely open. In a split second I was out of my body and quite aware of the experience. Our bedroom was alive with a misty white haze. Just four feet away, the burgundy-colored chest of drawers was barely visible and a scene was developing in the haze between me and the chest.

As I viewed through the haze, a profound scalloped orb traveled up in front of my eyes. It was pure silver and kept moving upward at an angle. It was that same shimmering silver that I saw when my friend, Jerry, greeted me in spiritual form in the middle of the night when he was dying. Obviously something was happening, but what? Had someone just died? Behind the orb, there were other smaller round orbs that looked like stars glowing in the background. And there were hundreds of them. It was one of those other-worldly scenes that took my breath away. As quickly as I was pulled out of my body, I snapped back in. "Wow," I thought. What was that? Who was that? I knew that the orb represented a person in spiritual form. That was a given. I made note of the fact that this all took place at precisely 6:00 AM.

As usual, at that place in our schedules, Dan and I passed in the hallway, so to speak. I fed the dogs and walked them. Dan was fussing in the kitchen and pondering what to make for breakfast. Once I was dressed to go to the office, our conversational moments were always over a relaxing morning meal. But I had just witnessed something important. To me the image was obviously about the fact that someone had died and was being installed in some eternal place. The shimmering silver was my connection with the spiritual place and literally told me that.

Amidst our mutual chatter, just so the event would be written on our symbolic family blackboard, I announced to Dan, "There was a spirit in our room this morning. In all likelihood, someone has died and I want to make a note of it even though I know nothing." Dan quietly acknowledged me and we went on with our meal. The only person who came to mind was my good friend, Neil who had passed two weeks earlier. But somehow the lag in time didn't fit. So we just let the information sit on the imaginary family blackboard until if, or when, information came our way.

And come it did. I was getting ready to go to to the office on the following Monday morning when the phone rang. Dan was deeply engaged in conversation with the spouse of our friend Perry, the physician. It was Perry who died at two AM that Thursday morning and I had my experience at six.

Perry and I had experienced many conversations about "other dimensions and even clairvoyant communication." We were great friends. He would almost shake with anger and get red in the face when I mentioned religion, but he always acknowledged that these other dimensions existed and that there was more to existence than what we could see feel and touch. There is no doubt in my mind that what I witnessed that morning; what he showed me, was his journey into eternity. He came to tell me that regardless of what we believe, our consciousness never dies.

REFERENCES

(1) The Encyclopedia of Mental Disorders, Dissociation

(2) Daniel J. Siegel, M.D., Mindsight, the New Science of Personal Transformation, Bantam Dell Pub. Group January 12, 2010

(3) Daniel J. Siegel M.D., Lecture, Evolution of Psychotherapy Conference, Milton Erickson Institute, December 2013

(4) A. Akimov, Ph.D., Torsion Fields, A New Science of Energy News, V.4, pp 11-14

(5) Claude Swanson, Ph.D., The Synchronized Universe, Posidea Press, 2009

(6) Wilhelm Reich, Ph.D., The Orgone Accumulator Handbook, The Biophysics of Orgone Energy, p 11

(7) Rupert Sheldrake, Ph.D. Morphic Fields – An Introduction

(8) Dean I. Radin, Ph.D., The Conscious Universe, The Scientific Truth About Psychic Phenomena, Harper-Collins Publishers, 1997, pp 174

(9) Kendra Cherrry, Consciousness; The Psychology of Awareness in Very Well, updated June 22, 2017

(10) The Daily Mail, March 8, 2017, Is There Really Life After Death?

(11) Ernest R. Rossi, Ph.D., The Collected Papers of Milton H. Erickson, V. 1, pp 452-477

(12) The American Psychiatric Association, The Diagnostic and Statistical Manual V

(13) Michio Kaku, Ph.D., Are There Other Universes? You Tube

(14) Wikipedia, The Akashic Record

(15) Bob Mitchell, Jason Quitt, Forbidden Knowledge; Revelations of a Multi-dimensional Time Traveler, Pub. Create Space Independent Publishing Platform, 2010

(16) Michael Talbot, The Holographic Universe, Harper-Collins Publishers, Great Britain, 1996, pp 75, 78

(17) Philippe Guillemant, The Road of Time; Theory of Double Causality,

(18) The Llewellyn Journal, An Interview with author Sara Wiseman, New Worlds of Body, Mind and Spirit, 2017

(19) Judith Orloff, M.D. Ten Traits Empathic People Share, Psychology Today, Feb. 19, 2016

(20) Bruce Lipton, Ph.D. The Biology of Belief: Unleashing the Power of Consciousness, Matter and Miracles, pub. March 18, 2005, By Mountain of Love